THE SOUTHERN WA...

CONTENTS

© Kevin Robertson (Noodle Books) and the various contributors 2013

ISBN 978-1-906419-94-3

First published in 2012 by Kevin Robertson

under the **NOODLE BOOKS** imprint

PO Box 279

Corhampton

SOUTHAMPTON

SO32 3ZX

www.noodlebooks.co.uk

editorial@thesouthernway.co.uk

Printed in England by

Berforts Information Press

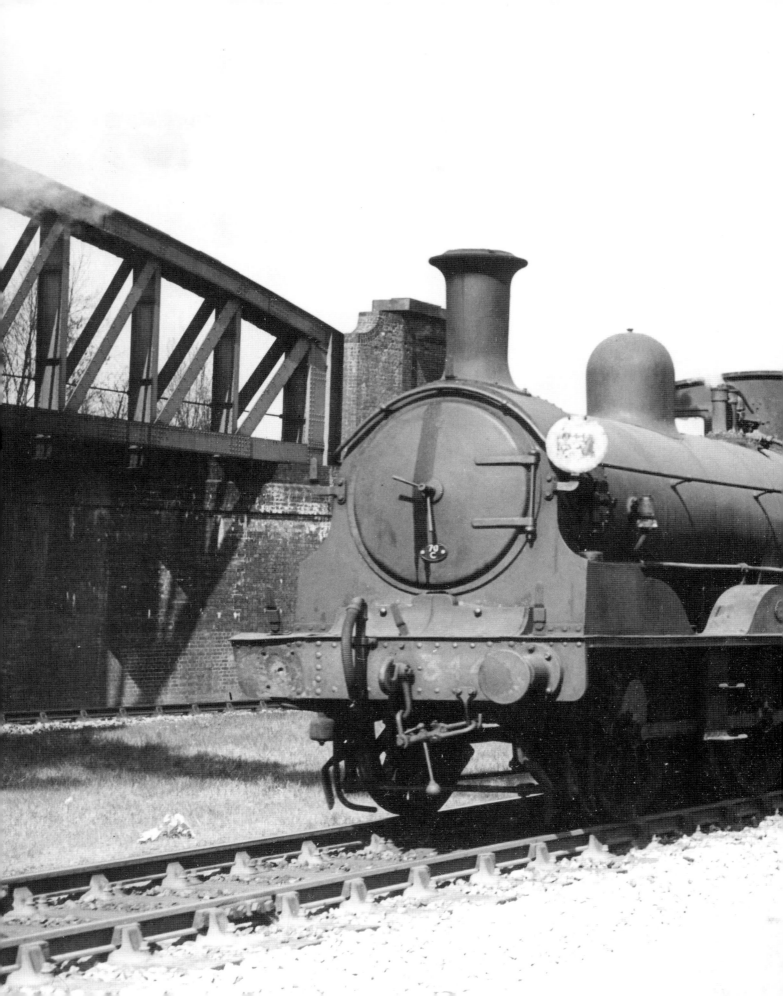

Front cover - Leaking steam from places where it probably shouldn't, No 34064 'Fighter Command' leaves Andover, London bound. The shape of the geisel ejector can just be made out atop the casing.

Pages 2 and 3 - Not a good day for the Southern Region. The 'Merchant Navy' has clearly failed and is being towed south past Worting Junction towards Eastleigh - minus a rod or two, whilst poor old No. 3441 looks as if it may have come off worst in a recent contretemps.

Above - The Southern Region at Brighton, steam and electric in harmony. Antony Ford collection.

Opposite page - Clapham, on a unreported date but clearly during the tenure of the 'overhead' on the Brighton side. 'A' box is in the background, but what an absolutely stunning signal-bridge in the foreground. The signals include: Windsor lines to the WLR, to up main and from up main to the Windsor lines and WLR. David Wallis collection.

(This particular negative was loaned with the comment, "See what, if anything you can make of that…." - there being a solid mass of what might well have been paint in the centre of the glass negative, although fortunately not on the emulsion side. Judicious use of the best kitchen knife - don't tell Mrs Robertson - a few choice expletives, a sore back, and several sessions later…… . it was just too good not to spend the effort upon.)

Rear cover - Seventy years ago, regular reader and friend Chris Watts was photographed by his family travelling on a wartime SR service, the image used on the rear cover of 'Southern Way Special No 6 Wartime Southern Part 3'. Rummaging recently through his papers, Chris came across the exact same magazine he had been reading all those years ago. It was too good an opportunity to miss! With grateful thanks also to Rodney Youngman.

Guest Editorial

This month's Guest editorial comes from the hand of Jeremy English, a friend it has been a privilege to know 'since before the last millennia'. I am sure many will have gone 'ooohhh' and aaahhhh' in the past over the production of some of his excellent video films as well as the renowned *Railscene* series. It has been a pleasure to welcome him into the 'Southern Way' fold.

"The first appearance of incredible material from the Michael Brooks collection of Southern ephemera (pages 74 to 82 and also accompanying the 'Lynton & Barnstaple article) in this issue of Southern Way, leads me to reflect on a gloomy scenario which I contemplated some 30 years ago when trying to find some railway films to watch on my then newly-acquired video recorder. There were at the time only about three available. Dissatisfied with these limited offerings I resolved to try and find more, which quickly led me to the British Transport Films archive. At the time no-one at the BTF had any plans to do anything with their material, the films themselves currently stored in arches under some obscure station. The staff though were very helpful, stating I could do what I wanted with them. I thus copied the material on to video with the intention of making it available to all.

"Whilst enthused at first, gloom quickly followed for I could not see any future beyond these BFT films. I felt that, by its very nature, archive film was a finite resource and thus a poor basis on which to build a business. Hence I decided to dribble the material out in conjunction with newly-shot contemporary footage and to present it in a style similar to printed magazines. Thus was born *Railscene,* the video magazine. Fortunately the idea took off quite rapidly and I was soon contacted by other enthusiasts, some of whom had access to other archive film, notably one Mike Arlett, who enquired if I might be interested in turning the films of a certain Ivo Peters into video.... ?

"That was my first indication there was indeed high-quality archive outside the BTF and crying out for a wider audience. More followed, Geoff Holyoake, Richard Willis, Eddie Stanbridge - and Patrick Whitehouse, the latter with his legendary 'Railway Roundabout' films. And today there are still films galore to be seen….(I am currently in talks to 'mine' an archive which has in excess of 2,000 hours of film!)

"All of which is also just as relevant to the still image as to the moving one, perhaps even more so. Kevin is forever coming across photographs of breathtaking quality and depth of knowledge. This material shows different aspect of Southern history which has barely been touched on previously and is absolutely fascinating. I have been privileged to see the initial scans of photographs of Southern history (below and pages 52/53), featuring mostly signalling and stations all of which illustrate aspects of the railway from the earliest days of its existence and which are mind-boggling in their extent.

"I am pleased to admit I was wrong - there's so much more archive still to come: whatever will we see next? Station Cats of the Southern?!"

Jeremy English

'Battle of Britain' 4-6-2 No. 34088, '213 Squadron', hurries through Sevenoaks with a Victoria-Dover Marine boat train. The leading vehicle is one of the Maunsell-designed 'Continental' 2nd class coaches introduced in 1924 for boat train traffic, although by this time it could be labelled 2nd or 3rd depending upon demand. 5 July 1959.

A E Bennett / The Transport Treasury

THE SEVENOAKS CUT-OFF

Jeremy Clarke

It may seem idiosyncratic that any description of this South Eastern Railway line should begin with the London & Croydon, even less excusably with the London & Brighton. For those idiosyncrasies one has to blame Parliament: short-termism in the Legislature is evidently no modern phenomenon!

The South Eastern's original independent route from London to Dover proposed in 1835 received the Royal Assent the next year. However, matters conspired to cause such dramatic alterations to that line that much of it was effectively abandoned. Its first part was instead to make use of the London & Croydon Railway to a point south of Norwood, later modified to be nearer Penge, before veering away to tunnel through the North Downs above Oxted to head for Tonbridge and The Weald.

This was not the first railway proposed through Kent to the Channel Coast, for on 21st December 1824 'The Times' published a full prospectus for "The Kentish Railway". The route from London to Dover and Sandwich was to be via Woolwich, Chatham and Canterbury with branches to Maidstone and Margate. Another scheme was mooted in 1832, being of especial interest because it planned to use train ferries to cross the Medway at Rochester and to Sheerness. Neither of these came to fruition of course though parts of both were integral to later schemes.

The London & Croydon Railway had been sanctioned on 5th June 1835 and opened four years later to the day. In the meantime the several promoters in the London & Brighton field, of whom oddly enough the South Eastern was at first one, had had their various proposals and lines examined by a Government-appointed engineer. Despite some underhand lobbying as well as pretty spiteful and insulting, not to say libellous, exchanges among the protagonists, he recommended the most direct route as we know it today which had been surveyed by Sir John Rennie. The L&BR was authorised on 15th July 1837. That authority was the cause of the South Eastern's change of route to the London & Croydon, the Act for it being passed the same year.

The SER line from the later junction at Penge was shown to run closely parallel to the Brighton line at least as far as Purley, a distance of some six miles, before it turned more toward the south east to climb the dip slope of the North Downs above Caterham. However, Parliament later considered that traffic offering would not warrant such an arrangement and therefore inserted a clause in the Brighton Bill to the effect that that company's line should be shared instead, arguing its case on both cost and, surprisingly perhaps for the time, environmental grounds, despite protests from both parties. But Parliament also offered a juicy carrot

to the South Eastern by stating the company might, at a later date, purchase at cost price the part of the Brighton line between that company's junction with the London & Croydon at Norwood and a relocated junction with its own realigned route 'north of Earlswood Common'. The South Eastern acceded to these changes but in 1839 Parliament, brooking no argument, amended the proposal yet again. Now, the line between Norwood and 'north of Earlswood Common' - which became Reigate Junction and which we know today as Redhill - was to be built by the two companies jointly. The Brighton actually did the work, the SER contributing £327,334, half the cost, although it still could, under the terms of the Brighton Act, have purchased the whole twelve miles between Norwood and Redhill. And there is where the trouble started.

Although this part of the line was funded as a joint venture it was not operated jointly. Instead the section was divided between the two, the Brighton retaining ownership of the northern half between Norwood and Stoats Nest (Coulsdon), the SER taking on the other half – the more expensive half! - through the North Downs to Redhill. By doing so the South Eastern had control of the junction where its Dover line turned away eastwards and was not slow in taking full advantage of it to the dismay of the Brighton. Uproar over priorities continued to dog the relationship between the two companies even after the new main line through Sevenoaks had opened and still carried on, if to a lesser extent, beyond 1899 when the Brighton managed to by-pass Redhill altogether on completion of the Quarry Line. Only Grouping ultimately resolved the problem.

The London & Brighton opened between Norwood and Haywards Heath on 12th July 1841 and throughout to Brighton on 21st September. The South Eastern line from Redhill reached Tonbridge (then spelt Tunbridge incidentally) on 25th May 1842, got to Headcorn on 31st August and Ashford on 1st December. There is barely a 'kink' worth the name from dead straight in the whole 47 miles of this section though a number of stations are thus placed well away from the towns and villages they purport to serve.

The next stage took the railway immediately to the west of the Foord stream in Folkestone by 28th June 1843. (Folkestone Central station opened here but not until 1884 and then as Cheriton Arch, renamed Radnor Park in 1886 and then to its present title in June 1895.) It was to be another six months after getting to this point before track crossed the nineteen arches of the majestic 100' high Foord viaduct and reached Folkestone Junction. By that time the company's engineer, William Cubitt, was already wrestling with the peculiar geological strata that make up the six-and-a-half

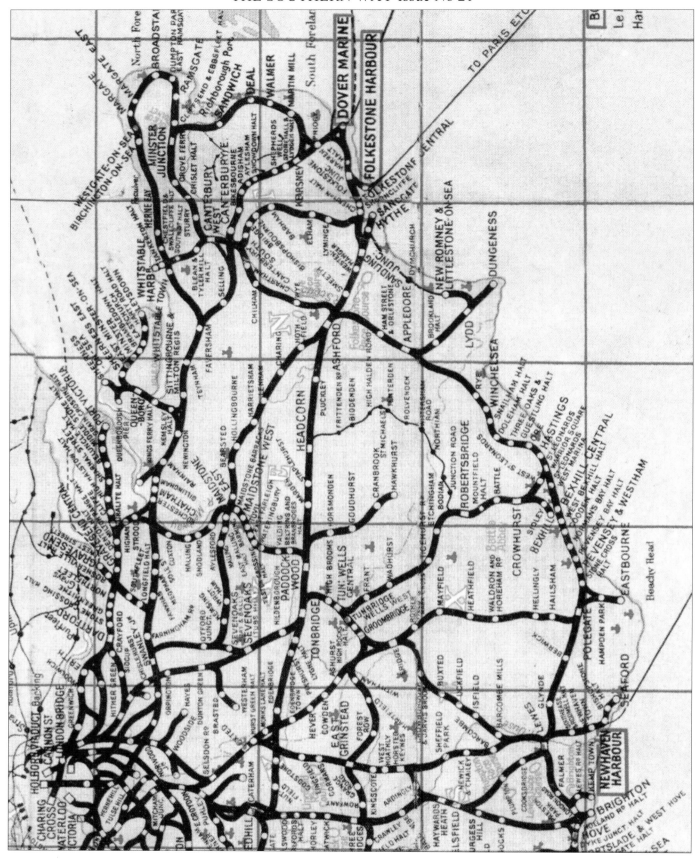

BR 'Standard' '7MT' class 4-6-2 No. 70004 'William Shakespeare', in pristine Stewarts Lane finish, passes Tonbridge on the through line with the down 'Golden Arrow'.

Prof. H P White / The Transport Treasury

miles between Folkestone and Dover, by far the most difficult and costly part of the whole route.

In the course of this section lie three tunnels, Martello (530 yds), Abbotscliffe (sic) (1 mile 182 yds) and Shakespeare Cliff (1,387 yds). Martello tunnel, though the shortest of the three, proved the most difficult to construct because it straddles the ridge that separates The Weald from the undercliff next to the sea. The layers of gault clay and greensand that lie beneath the chalk of the North Downs, which are curving here toward the coast to form the 'White Cliffs', rise to the surface at this location making tunnelling or cutting both difficult and expensive. The tunnel required lining with six rings of brick.

From the eastern end of Martello tunnel to Abbotscliffe tunnel the track traverses the one-and-three-quarter miles of Folkestone Warren, another geological jumble that has seen several landslips of varying severity over the years, some serious enough to close the section until work to stabilise it and repair the damage had been completed. The most notable occurred on 19th December 1915 when virtually the whole length of the Warren shifted up to 50 yards nearer the sea. The section remained closed until 1919, the passenger train passing through at the time of the slip being stranded together with its locomotive until then.

Abbotscliffe tunnel was driven from galleries dug into the cliff from a road overlooking the Channel as well as by the more conventional method of headings from vertical shafts. The galleries permitted chalk spoil from the workings to be wheeled out and tipped directly into the sea. This tunnel is also brick lined for its whole length.

Shakespeare Cliff presented different problems, for the chalk here is both unstable and friable. For these reasons two parallel single-line tunnels were bored about ten feet

apart, each in the form of a narrow, pointed Gothic arch to a height of 27½ feet at the Folkestone end and no less than 29 feet at the Dover end. In this form the pressures just below the head of the arch are inward rather than downward and so held by the acute apex. The portals are faced in brick and the tunnel walls retained by a lining six bricks thick.

But Cubitt also had to contend with the great chalk bluff of Round Down cliff lying between the two longer tunnels and rising to a height of about 375 feet above high tide level. The line to be taken here showed the outer wall of any tunnel at this point would be at most only seventy feet thick and for much of the way rather less. Given the unstable nature of the chalk, Cubitt concluded that tunnelling would be impractical and making a cutting out of the question. He therefore decided to remove the whole cliff using explosives, an action that to today's environmentalists would seem nothing short of officially-sanctioned vandalism on a huge scale. Following advice he handed responsibility for this to a Royal Engineers officer, Lieut. Hutchinson, who placed about 18,000lbs of gunpowder in three separate charges within the base of the cliff.

An expectant crowd had gathered on 26th January 1843 to witness what they anticipated would be a show of unimaginable pyrotechnics. Lieut. Hutchinson disappointed them. As 'The Times' described it, '..... *a low, faint rumble was heard and immediately afterwards the bottom of the cliff began to belly out and then, almost simultaneously .... the summit began to sink. There was no roaring explosion, no bursting out of fire, no violent or crushing splitting of rocks .....*' The efficient Hutchinson had set off his three accurately weighed and placed charges simultaneously by electricity, possibly the first recorded instance of detonation by such means. Nowadays this section is strung with trip wires on the down side to warn of any chalk falls that could

Tonbridge-allocated 'H' class 0-4-4T No. 31523 stands with the Westerham branch push/pull train on the run-round loop at Dunton Green. The train itself, possibly set No. 481 which worked the branch for many years, consists of the carriage portion of former SECR railcars. Prof. H P White / The Transport Treasury

block the track and to set approach signals automatically to 'danger'.

On the way into Dover Cubitt took the line along the foreshore, constructing a timber trestle bridge built on piles sunk into the underlying chalk and to a height above the water that, according to the Board of Trade's Inspecting Officer ....'[will] *prevent them from being injured by the sea* [and] *at the same time the tides have no tendency to wash away the beach ....*' The completed route, 89 miles long, opened to the original Dover Town station on 7th February 1844, three years before construction of the Admiralty Pier commenced. (The trestle lasted until 1927 when Dover's Archcliffe Fort was demolished and other alterations were being undertaken in the vicinity. This part of the line now runs on an embankment behind a substantial sea wall.)

The South Eastern enjoyed and was so confident of continuing its monopoly of Continental traffic it failed to recognise the possible threat posed by an impecunious and parochial concern that had put down rather uncertain roots at the SER station at Strood. The South Eastern had got here by

opening a line from Gravesend on 23rd August 1847, taking over much of the route of the Thames & Medway Canal in the process. The canal owners had earlier laid a single line of rails on the towpath through the 2¼ miles of tunnel between Higham and Strood. (Sections of the canal, now little more than ditches and much overgrown in places, are extant.)

The South Eastern drained the canal in the tunnel and used the channel to form the trackbed. Two years later the company completed this line through North Kent with the opening of the section from North Kent East Junction, west of Deptford station on the venerable London & Greenwich Railway, via Woolwich and Dartford to an end-on junction with the Strood line at Gravesend. The suburban part of the route was necessarily circuitous as the Royal Observatory at Greenwich had successfully prevented extension eastward from Greenwich itself on the grounds the vibration caused by the trains would affect its delicate instruments. Instead the line turned south east at North Kent East Junction before describing a quarter-circle through Lewisham, Blackheath and Charlton, well away from the Observatory though, if some of the scientists were to be believed, still not nearly far enough. (The missing Greenwich-Charlton bit had to wait almost another thirty years, completed in two stages, Charlton-Maze Hill 1/1/73, Greenwich-Maze Hill 1/2/78.)

In 1853 the East Kent Railway had obtained authorisation for a line to Canterbury from Strood. A 'Facilitation Clause' in the Act obliged the South Eastern to handle EKR London traffic there as expeditiously as it would its own, the East Kent having been refused running powers over the North Kent line. Now, with the EKR already building, the South Eastern sought authority to construct a line up the Medway Valley from Strood to make an end-on junction at Maidstone with its branch from Paddock Wood opened in 1844. Rather than insist that the SER lay down a few additional yards of parallel track at Strood the East Kent offered to share its own line for the very short distance to the point where the two routes diverged. By way of reciprocation the SER agreed without dissent a Lords' Committee directive it would not raise any objection to the East Kent seeking an Act to extend its line from Canterbury to Dover. One might, perhaps, charge the South Eastern Board with extraordinary naivety, maybe even with extraordinary arrogance on happily agreeing to this without giving thought to any expansionist aspirations the East Kent Railway might harbour. To press the point the shareholders were confidently told in 1849 that '.... *the company holds a natural position for handling land traffic between Europe and Great Britain and cannot be dispossessed of it'*. The fact is, of course, the SER saw the East Kent as nothing more than a convenient extension of its own North Kent line through the heart of the County which would generate receipts for the company at comparatively little expense.

The financially weak East Kent progressed very slowly. The section from Strood to Faversham opened on 29th March 1858 on completion of the bridge over the Medway (Chatham to Faversham had been opened two months previously), but it did not reach Canterbury until 9th July 1860, though powers to extend to Dover had been obtained in 1855. That final section opened on 22nd July 1861 to a station - now 'Priory' - rather closer to the town centre than the SER's ostensible 'Town' establishment, and to Dover Harbour itself on 1st November. But by that time the East Kent, though it retained rights of access, had uprooted itself and shaken the dust of Strood and the South Eastern off its corporate boots and from 3rd December 1860 got right into the heart of London. This had been achieved through running powers over the lines of the Mid-Kent Railway, the West End of London & Crystal Palace Railway and the Victoria Station & Pimlico Railway, and a new independent route of its own between Rochester Bridge and Bickley. This had been authorised in 1858 though, as already noted, the Dover line at that time was open only as far as Faversham. And as though to throw such independence in the face of the SER this impecunious and once parochial concern had metamorphosed into the London, Chatham & Dover Railway, a fierce rival for the next forty

years. The final part of the company's main line, between Herne Hill and Beckenham Junction, which permitted it to forsake the somewhat roundabout approach to London over the other companies' routes, was authorised in 1860 and opened on 1st July 1863, making the distance between London's Victoria station and Dover Priory just over 77¼ miles.

Suddenly finding it could, after all, be dispossessed of its natural position for handling all Continental traffic, the alarmed SER had fought the East Kent Bill ferociously, basically claiming another route into London from Kent was completely unnecessary. But the company, it seemed, had not learned that Parliament appeared to have a soft spot for the East Kent and had favoured its applications on a number of occasions, so much so it had acquired a reputation as 'the spoiled child of the legislature'. Thus the South Eastern may not necessarily have had only itself to blame for failure to prevent the Bill's passage, though with Parliamentary favouritism in mind a rather less 'head-on' and rather more subtle approach in its opposition might have been more effective.

On the other hand the company had from the start persistently delayed and obstructed East Kent traffic at Strood in the misplaced confidence of its own position and despite the agreed and legally binding 'Facilitation Clause'. Worse, in 1856 it had succeeded in blocking another EKR attempt to get running powers over the North Kent route via Gravesend to the start of an independent line into Victoria from Lewisham on the grounds that it did not have the necessary capacity. This argument had now come back to haunt it with a vengeance. The final straw from the South Eastern's point of view was that the interloper had a distance advantage of almost twelve miles between London and Dover though over a much more difficult route, crossing as it does the 'grain' of the land for much of the way as the briefest of glimpses at a gradient profile will testify.

In these circumstances many SER shareholders felt they had at the least been misled if not downright cheated by the short-sightedness and misplaced confidence of the Board. But then, had any of them expressed any doubt about the validity of the statement concerning the strength of the company's monopoly position made at that meeting in 1849, or indeed at any subsequent ones? Surely some of them ought to have harboured the thought there could be expansionist tendencies on the part of the East Kent. Or did they consider that in its parlous financial state it could soon be bought out at a very advantageous price to their benefit? Certainly a lack of imagination, maybe of business acumen may be laid at the door of the Boardroom. But it is extraordinary that no shareholder appears to have been any more imaginative or possessed of greater acumen except subsequently, with the benefit of twenty-twenty hindsight and when the value of their holdings dipped at the prospect of competition and a reduction of dividends threatened.

The unrest among them, especially that influential group based in Manchester with particularly large shareholdings, brought one of the most aggressive railwaymen of the time to the head of the SER board. Edward Watkin's rising career had started in 1845 with the Trent Valley Railway which he succeeded in selling to the acquisitive London & North Western at a very advantageous price to his employers. His success in that transaction was, perhaps, the reason he went to Euston to work for the piratical figure of Mark Huish. Thence to the Manchester, Sheffield & Lincolnshire Railway, a connection he retained even after the South Eastern, by some underhand lobbying among Board members, possibly prodded from Manchester, eased out one of its directors in 1864 to create a vacancy which Watkin was invited to fill. He joined the Board on 19th January 1865, became Deputy Chairman a month later and Chairman in March 1866. From that point on there were no holds barred in his dealings with the LCDR and its suave and clever spiv of a Chairman, James Staats Forbes. But it may be a significant pointer to Watkin's prickly, pugnacious and aggressive character that almost all litigation between the two companies, of which there was much and mainly instigated by him, was found in the Chatham's favour to the South Eastern's cost. Perhaps the Courts had as soft a spot for the LCDR as Parliament had! But then, knowing Watkin's reputation, probably not.

Even before Watkin's arrival however, moves were afoot to get the company's London terminus closer to both the City and the West End than the south bank site at London Bridge; this in response to the Chatham's station at Victoria and the soon-to-be-opened one at Ludgate Hill when the bridge over the Thames from Blackfriars had been completed. More significantly however, plans had already been drawn up to nullify the Chatham's distance advantage to Dover by building a line that formed a rough hypotenuse to the two sides of the London-Redhill-Tonbridge triangle.

The line from London Bridge to Charing Cross – known simply as The Charing Cross Railway - was promoted by an independent company and authorised in 1859. The SER Chairman, Hon. James Byng, secured shareholder agreement to invest £300,000 in the venture. But that contribution has to be seen in the context of an undertaking made by Byng to a House of Commons Committee in 1857 that he would call upon South Eastern shareholders to promote or support such a scheme. Not only would the line reach the West End but, to Parliamentary satisfaction, by a connection with the London & South Western at Waterloo, the West London Extension would also become accessible and, thereby, the Great Western and the London & North Western and all points north and west. A 'branch' from the Charing Cross line into Cannon Street received the Royal Assent in 1861. Amalgamation of the Charing Cross company with the SER was granted in 1863.

The Charing Cross Bill was strenuously opposed by the Brighton and even more so by the St Thomas's Hospital Governors and Trustees. The hospital was situated in Southwark High Street and the proposed route of the railway crossed a small corner of the grounds though it did not impinge on the buildings themselves. But such was the strength of the Trustees' objections a clause was inserted into the Bill which permitted the Hospital, if the Trustees so wished, to call on the company to buy all the grounds and the buildings despite the requirement of the SER being only ⅙ of an acre. As might have been anticipated, with the Bill passed ,the railway was immediately served with a demand they buy the whole site, the price asked being £750,000 though the capital of the Charing Cross Company then was only £50,000 more than this!

The dispute went to arbitration where the sum to be paid was eventually fixed at £296,000, that figure changing hands on 21st January 1862. Even then there was trouble with litigation being resorted to by both parties when the Trustees refused to permit access and the railway company's workmen forced their way in. Ultimately a compromise was agreed in which the railway could get to the portion of the grounds required for work to start while the Hospital could continue to use the remainder of the site until July that year. (As a reminder of former days St Thomas Street still runs east from Borough High Street below the south side of London Bridge station while the Charing Cross Railway's funds went to establish the present St Thomas's Hospital on the south bank of the Thames opposite the Palace of Westminster.)

Quite apart from the financial demands of St Thomas's the Charing Cross Railway proved a much more costly line than had originally been budgeted for. At the half-yearly meeting on 26th February 1863 shareholders were advised that traffic growth required three lines of rails to be provided against the two that had been planned. Moreover, in anticipation of further demand land would be purchased for a fourth line and a fifth where practicable. Hungerford Bridge would also be built four tracks wide from the outset and not two as the original drawings showed.

Local traffic from Greenwich and the Mid-Kent routes inaugurated Charing Cross on 11th January 1864. In conformity with Byng's promise a single line spur, which was usable from the same day, passed between platforms 2 and 3 (later 4 and 6, the spur itself then being classified as no 5) in the main part of the South Western's soon-to-be labyrinthine Waterloo station, crossed the concourse and bridged Waterloo Road to make a junction with what is now the down 'through' line of the Charing Cross Railway. North Kent trains began to serve Charing Cross from 1st April, main line services coming a month later.

On 1st January 1869 the South Eastern opened a new station at the point where the spur from Waterloo joined the Charing Cross line. Named originally Waterloo Junction it became Waterloo Eastern in July 1935 but has been Waterloo East since May 1977. From soon after Grouping the numbered platforms were lettered A to D instead to avoid confusion with the main station.

The LNWR inaugurated a Willesden Junction-London Bridge service over the spur in July 1865 which diverted into Cannon Street from 1st February 1867. But there was no arrangement for the North Western engine to work through so both the LSWR and SER had to provide locomotives for those parts of the journey over their respective metals. Not surprisingly the service proved hopelessly uneconomic and was withdrawn on 1st January 1868. Thereafter the spur never attracted any regular traffic, being used only sporadically for specials and exchange of vehicles. Certainly no efforts were ever made for the line to carry the sort of long distance inter-company traffic Parliament had envisaged. It was lost with the rebuilding of Waterloo, completed in 1922, though it had been severed before then. The bridge across Waterloo Road was later turned over to passenger use as a walkway between the two stations. In the meantime work had continued on the line to the very imposing Cannon Street station: it opened on 1st September 1866.

It has to be remembered that at this time, despite Byng's promise to promote or support a line to the West End, termini there were considered by the southern railway companies to be of lesser importance than those in the City. Thus Charing Cross is on a relatively narrow site and despite the imposing station hotel frontage has never had more than six platforms though there are now five approach tracks on Hungerford Bridge. Cannon Street by comparison had nine platforms and no fewer than ten tracks across the river. The reason for the latter is that from the time the station opened it was customary for trains between London Bridge and Charing Cross to work into and out of Cannon Street *en route*. Although that style of operation generally ceased early in the 20th century and the layout was completely and comprehensively reconfigured at the time of electrification in 1926, its legacy impinges directly on services today. The base of the triangle thus formed, between Borough Market Junction and Metropolitan Junction, least used then but the busiest section for many years now, is still only two tracks wide. But with the belated 'Thameslink Programme' at last making progress this bottleneck is on course to be widened to four lines though it seems Charing Cross trains will still have use of only two of them. A little relief will be forthcoming however by transfer of the four Thameslink trains each way each hour off-peak that presently require a path.

While the SER continued to work its way further into central London, the first section of the new hypotenuse via Sevenoaks, authorised in 1862, opened on 1st July 1865. It headed south eastwards for five-and-a-half miles from a junction with the North Kent line at St Johns, west of Lewisham station. This initial section terminated at Chislehurst, having tunnelled unnecessarily for 649 yards through a shallow ridge about one-and-a-quarter miles north of that station because the landowner refused access during construction. In places the tunnel roof is only four feet below the surface. Fourteen months on, a line to Dartford via Sidcup, later named the 'Dartford Loop', opened from a junction with this new main line at what later became Hither Green station (opened 1st June 1895), 1½ miles south of St Johns. Electrification from 6th June 1926 brought rapid

urban development and house building along its route on a massive scale over the next ten years or so.

The line thus far to Chislehurst has been climbing relentlessly out of the Thames Valley since St Johns, mostly at 1 in 140/120 though there is a short section of level track on the approach to the then terminus. But that is a barely noticeable respite on the 11-mile climb, for the line southwards now forsakes the London Clay and is well and truly on the dip slope of the chalk North Downs, making this one of the most difficult exits of any main line out of London. As far as Petts Wood from south of Grove Park, where it has metamorphosed into the Quaggy River, the route follows the valley of the small Kyd Brook, much of which is now culverted. But thereafter some very heavy earthworks were necessary. This was particularly so around Orpington and on to the summit a little way beyond Knockholt, just short of 17 miles from Charing Cross, the climb culminating with two miles at 1 in 120 which includes the twenty-seven chains of Chelsfield tunnel.

However, if the engineers thought this section presented problems they were as nothing to those posed by the scarp slope of the chalk Downs and the thrusting ridge of greensand that guards the northern edge of the High Weald. Here the two longest tunnels on the former Southern Railway were required as the line plunges down to the level of the River Medway at Tonbridge. The northerly tunnel, Polhill, driven for almost 1½ miles through the chalk, is immediately beyond the summit and carries the line down a 1 in 143 gradient through the first part of the fall on to gault clay in the valley of the River Darent at Dunton Green. There follows a 1¾ mile long climb at 1 in 160 through Sevenoaks on to the lower slopes of the greensand outcrop which is then pierced by the 1 mile 77 chains of Sevenoaks tunnel, downhill again at 1 in 144. From the south end of the tunnel the gradient sharpens, to 1 in 122 for four miles, until the line reaches the floor of the Medway valley and levels out on it for the last ¾ mile into Tonbridge. From St Johns to the meeting point with the original route from Redhill at Tonbridge West Junction the Sevenoaks cut-off is 24 miles and 50 chains long, making an overall saving of 12½ miles.

The line from Chislehurst opened to the public as far as Sevenoaks on 3rd March 1868. Local services got to Tonbridge on 1st May though main line trains were not switched to the new route for another month. The South Eastern continued to run passenger services via Redhill though as time passed these not unnaturally took on a local rather than an express character. However, much of the slower freight traffic continued to be sent this way so as to avoid taking up available paths through the Downs.

Quadrupling of the line between New Cross and Orpington was undertaken from 1902 and completed in June 1905. In the course of this all stations had to be rebuilt, a pleasant and generous if simple style being adopted for the most part. Driving the new tunnel required north of Chislehurst caused damage to the original, necessitating its closure between July and November 1903 while repairs were

Maunsell 'V' class 4-4-0 No. 30905, 'Tonbridge', heads the 3.25 pm Charing Cross to Hastings train at Chislehurst. The first two coaches are former SECR 100-seaters: a slab-sided Maunsell 8' 0½" - wide set from 1928 follows. Several sets as well as a number of 'loose' coaches were built to this restricted width because of the tight cleaances in the tunnels south of Tunbridge Wells. 'Chislehurst Goods' signalbox may be seen in the middle distance to the left of the train while the 'cleared' signal applies to the up slow line, to its right. 6 April 1955.   *R C Riley / The Transport Treasury*

effected.   Over this period a number of services were diverted via Oxted, the Crowhurst Junctions and Edenbridge as well as making more use of the original route via Redhill.

Electrification of the 'cut-off' came about in stages: the Southern Railway electrified Charing Cross and Cannon Street to Orpington from 28th February 1926 and Orpington to Sevenoaks on 6th January 1935. (As an indication of its influence on living and travelling habits, the population of Orpington, just over 4,000 at the beginning of the 20th century, had increased to almost 10,000 by 1931.) The section from Sevenoaks to Tonbridge formed part of Phase 2 of the Kent Coast Electrification Scheme as contained in the Modernisation Plan of 1955, though the Southern had already earmarked it in 1946 and, indeed before then. The full electrified service for this phase came into operation on 18th June 1962.

More radical track changes were made as commissioning of the London Bridge Control Centre

progressed from 1976. The principal objective was to segregate Charing Cross- and Cannon Street-bound trains well to the east of London Bridge rather than at Borough Market Junction as had been the case up to this time. St Johns and New Cross both lost their main line platforms which, in the case of the former, gave room for the 'through' tracks to be straightened with a commensurate rise in the speed limit, and at the latter permitted an extra line to be laid through the station. Also as part of these changes a bi-directional single-track spur was constructed to join the down Nunhead-Lewisham line - which also became bi-directional for the short distance to the up end of Lewisham station - to a double junction on the fast lines at the north end of St Johns. This permits Charing Cross trains to get to and from Lewisham and points south and east without having to cross any other lines on the level. It opened on 29th March 1976. Under current plans this spur is due to be doubled.

West of New Cross the former 'down no. 2' line became reversible right through from the station to the west

14

end of London Bridge. This formation solved a problem. Cannon Street had very little traffic outside rush hours, which made the provision of four tracks serving it unjustifiable. On the other hand it needed more than a single line in each direction at those busy times. This bi-directional track between up and down lines and thereby immediately accessible from both provided the answer. By contrast Charing Cross traffic required all the track provision it could get throughout the day and particularly in rush hours. To this end another line was added to the formation inward from Blue Anchor Junction, 1½ miles out of London Bridge, by transferring the Brighton down main slow to the South Eastern side. This line, used in the up direction, also goes right through to the west end of London Bridge but has never had a platform at that station. However, because of the Thameslink project this also is due to change. Further operational flexibility was provided by making the lines through London Bridge platform nos. 3, 4 and 5 as well as no. 2 reversible.

Borough Market Junction ceased to exist then as a functioning entity though for some years a connection remained between the Charing Cross and Cannon Street lines in the up direction for emergency purposes. On the very few occasions it was used it proved embarrassingly difficult to keep a train on the rails due to the very sharp curvature and slightly adverse cant and was later removed.

Finally, sets of medium-speed crossovers were installed at Spa Road Junction, one mile from London Bridge, by which Charing Cross trains calling at New Cross and St Johns as well as those to/from the Greenwich line could reach the appropriate side of the layout. There are, however, limited facilities for movements from one side of the formation to the other at the east end of London Bridge though their use is rare.

The Sevenoaks line effectively begins at Blue Anchor where the Brighton Line turns away southward. Less than a mile further on is North Kent East Junction, 4¼ miles from Charing Cross: the Greenwich line goes straight ahead at this point, thus clearly showing which route is the later arrival. The first signalbox at the junction was superseded by another in 1929 when the whole area out of London Bridge was re-signalled with colour-lights. That box, a typical SER-style timber building, sat atop a steel girder frame on brick piers straddling the Greenwich line just south of the bridge over the now long-gone Surrey Canal. It lasted until the first stage of the London Bridge re-signalling scheme came on stream in 1976.

New Cross station is 4 m. 68 chains from Charing Cross and opened with the line. The original building with its rendered brick and stone facade facing New Cross Road suffered considerable damage in wartime and steady dilapidation subsequently. It was demolished in 1975 when new glass and steel buildings were provided on the down side at the same time as the platform side of the station was being rebuilt.

Connections on both sides with the East London

Line were laid in at New Cross in 1880. That line was electrified from 31st March 1913, its own passenger services then becoming self-contained though goods and special traffic continued to run over it. In 1933 it became part of London Transport but continued to carry other traffic until connections with the main line here and at New Cross Gate station on the Brighton line were severed in the 1970s. The line is now part of London Overground whose trains, which at the time of writing, run as far north as Highbury & Islington, continue to use the down side bay at New Cross. Connections for through working to West Croydon and Crystal Palace have been re-established at New Cross Gate. From New Cross southwards the four tracks are presently classified by pairs, 'slow' and 'fast', the former being to the east until merger south of Orpington.

Thus far the railway has been on brick arches, the legacy of the London & Greenwich Railway's elevated entry into the capital. New Cross is the first point since leaving Charing Cross at which the Sevenoaks line reaches ground level. Not for long however, for immediately after passing under the New Cross Road bridge at the south end of the station the line is in cutting and making a brief climb at 1 in 191 to a summit at the north end of the short Tanners Hill tunnel. Widening is obvious here for in addition to substantial retaining walls being required to hold up the cut-back sides of the cutting, a single line tunnel was bored each side of the original double line one to take the additional tracks.

St Johns station (5m 47ch) opened on 1st June 1873, the track layout at the junction at the south end showing again that the Sevenoaks line was the late-comer as it swings sharply away south eastwards from the original North Kent route to Lewisham and Blackheath. St Johns signalbox, also commissioned in 1929, stood on the down side right by the junction. It too closed in 1976. After the 1902 widening the station had two island platforms, the one for the fast lines requiring the up one to negotiate a quite violent and speed-restricted reverse curve around its outer face. This platform was removed in September 1973 permitting the curves to be eliminated. There is neither goods yard nor road access to this station, entry being by a steel girder footbridge over the track from St John's Vale at the up end. Ticketing facilities are available at the foot of the steps to the platform.

The line now begins to climb in earnest, at first on a long reverse curve at a gradient of 1 in 200/250. Before reaching Parks Bridge Junction there are two heavily speed-restricted crossovers from west to east between the 'fast and 'slow' lines. Parks Bridge Junction itself is the point at which the Mid-Kent Railway between Lewisham and Ladywell passes beneath the main line on its way to Hayes. The Mid-Kent's first phase opened from Lewisham to Beckenham Junction in January 1857. A double-track spur on the up side at Parks Bridge, the Ladywell Loop, connects the fast lines to the Mid-Kent: it opened in September 1866. Parks Bridge Junction signalbox, another closed in 1976, stood on the down side close to the Mid-Kent bridge.

The signalman in the isolated 'Polhill Intermediate' box sees 'N15' class 4-6-0 No. 30798, 'Sir Hectimere', climbing easily toward the steeper gradient through Polhill tunnel and to the summit at Knockholt with an up van train for London bridge. Note the tall co-acting down signal positioned on the outside of the curve for ease of sighting. 9 April 1955.

R C Riley / The Transport Treasury

A second double track connection, the Courthill Loop, rises steeply on a sharp curve from the Lewisham side of the Mid-Kent to join the slow lines. This was opened by the Southern Railway in 1929 as part of a scheme to reroute the heavy cross-London freight traffic to and from Hither Green yards via Snow Hill away from the route through London Bridge. This had seen a considerable rise in track occupation since electrification, making freight pathing very difficult. A proportion of that traffic continued to traverse this route off-peak however, climbing the spur used now by Thameslink trains from Metropolitan Junction to Blackfriars Junction to reach Snow Hill tunnel and the Widened Lines at Farringdon. But after the change most got to Farringdon via a new causeway from Lewisham that joined the west end of the re-opened ex-LCDR Greenwich Park branch (closed 1st January 1917) to Nunhead. From there it travelled the Catford Loop to Loughborough Junction to be routed thence via the Metropolitan Extension Line to Blackfriars and Snow Hill. As a bonus, use of the Catford Loop permitted direct access to the West London Line from Factory Junction (Battersea), thus much easing transfer of freight traffic to and from the Great Western and LMS that had previously been exchanged less conveniently elsewhere.

Beyond Parks Bridge the gradient sharpens to 1 in 140. Hither Green station is 7m. 16 ch. from Charing Cross, the junction with the Dartford Loop being at the up end, and in this case it is that line which curves sharply away toward the east. The wide trackbed between the two Loop platforms shows there were once three lines here. The now-trackless space in the centre is where freight trains waited for a path towards Lewisham and Nunhead. Its line was lifted in the early 1980s when wagonload traffic ceased. The fast lines retain their platforms as indeed do those at all the stations southward to Orpington.

An entrance was provided at the northern end of the station which is still the case. Since 1974 the booking office has been at platform level in the 'V' between the diverging routes and is approached up a ramp from a public pedestrian subway – which has the Greenwich Meridian marked on its arch - beneath the railway. But the developer of the estate on the west side of the line paid for another building and entrance at the south end of the up main platform. This was a typical SER construction in lapped timber with a low-pitched slated roof and a generous roadside canopy the length of the building. This no longer exists though the entrance is still used during rush hours.

The down side of the station had a signalbox at each end, 'A' box to the north of the Dartford Loop junction, 'B' box at the south end of the slow line platform. Both closed in February 1962 when a new panel box was commissioned. That closed in November 1976 when its duties were taken over by the London Bridge control centre.

Hither Green is synonymous with marshalling yards. These were located south of the station, first laid down in 1899. Three signalboxes classified Hither Green Sidings 'A', 'B' and 'C' and spread over their length on the

up side from north to south governed movements in and out of the yards. They also closed in February 1962. The nearby loco depot was opened on the down side by the Southern in 1933. This was a single-ended, six-road shed which included a wheel-drop. To the east a raised coal stage at which four engines could be coaled at once was approached by a ramp and had a 65' turntable located beyond it. As might be expected freight locomotives figured predominantly in the shed's allocation but passenger engines were not unknown there. In 1947 for example, on the eve of Nationalisation, of the fifty-five engines on the books six were 4-4-0s, three each of classes B1 and F1, former SER Stirling-designed engines re-boilered by Wainwright. For a while in the late-1950s the depot could boast a single 'King Arthur' in its allocation, nos. 30799, *Sir Ironside* and 30806, *Sir Galleron* filling the post at various times. Classified 73C by BR and extant, though now housing and servicing diesel locomotives, the shed is set in a triangle of lines completed by a double-track chord, the Lee Spur, coming in off the Dartford Loop. Once clear of the shed precincts the slow lines throw off two tracks to the down marshalling yard: the Lee Spur makes a south facing junction with these. The 1962 panel box was located on the down side close to the shed outlet.

Five sidings in the revamped yard site are still allotted to freight traffic though no marshalling takes place here now. Eight more sidings with two washers berth "southeastern" 'Networker' electric stock as part of the longstanding Grove Park depot complex with access additionally at the down end. The up yard, also of eight sidings with a washer, performs a similar berthing function. As with the down yard this is accessible at both ends by connections with the up through line, the northern end of this yard being on the site of the holding sidings and approach roads for the former Continental Freight Depot opened in October 1960. Those lines were equipped with overhead wiring to power pantograph-equipped electric locomotives off the third rail. Despite its relatively close position to Central London and immediate access to the South Circular Road the depot rarely - if ever! - worked to capacity. Merchants later found it more convenient to unload the long-wheelbase 4-wheel ferry wagons at sidings out in rural Kent which had and still has easy access to improved major roads and the motorway network, rather than to expect their vehicles to pick their way safely through this densely trafficked area of South East London. The depot closed in February 1987 and was demolished the following year.

The gradient steepens to 1 in 120 with a brief intermission at 1 in 75 on the approach to Grove Park where a large housing estate was built between the wars on behalf the London County Council. A contractor's siding to bring in building materials trailed in to the up fast line and was in use between June 1924 and May 1937.

A six-road carriage shed on the down side precedes the station. This shed was first constructed in 1926 to house and maintain electric stock: five more open sidings are laid alongside it, three to the east, two to the west. Carriage washing and maintenance facilities continue to be provided here.

Grove Park station, opened on 1st November 1871 and part paid for by the local landowner, is a couple of chains short of nine miles from Charing Cross. The building in brick is on the Baring Road bridge at the north end. This station is the junction for the Bromley North branch which curves away southward at the down end. Financed locally and opened on 1st January 1878, the owning company was absorbed the following year by the South Eastern, which had worked the branch from the beginning.

There are a two island platforms at this station, one serving the slow lines, the other the fast ones. But there is also an apparent additional 'island' platform between the spur from the branch and the up fast line. However, it is cut back from and fenced against the latter to form a single-faced platform for branch services. At one time the down end at Grove Park was riddled with points and diamond crossings to permit access to and from the branch but these were all removed in 1961 as part of phase 2 of the Kent Coast electrification scheme and a single down direction fast-slow crossover installed. There are no through workings on the branch at all now and the only connection with the main line remains at the up end of the branch platform and that to cater only for empty stock working.

A signalbox with 31 levers provided at the widening in 1905 and sited in the divergence was destroyed by fire in 1938. A new box on the same site with a 60-lever frame was commissioned just twelve days later. Other than a single siding on the west side of the station there were no goods facilities here though a bank of five sidings with a headshunt occupied land to the east. They were used mainly for off-peak stock storage and lasted into the 1970s but were never electrified. The site is now covered by a small housing estate.

Immediately on passing Grove Park the line enters a shallow cutting that would, but for the recalcitrance of the local landowner, have continued through to Elmstead Woods station. It also marks the point at which the London Bridge Control Centre relinquishes its duties to its counterpart at Ashford. The fast lines use the newer of the two tunnels, on the west side and 591 yards long. Only a quarter of a mile from the southern exit the route reaches the station. This was another latecomer, opened with the widening as Elmstead in July 1904, the addendum appearing from 1st October 1908. The brick station building is on the down side and has stone round-headed window frames and a shallow-ridged slated roof. The lattice footbridge to the other two platforms stands just north of it. The up fast platform, unused except in an emergency or when maintenance closes the slow lines, is now devoid of buildings and its very generous canopy. No goods yard was provided here. The small signalbox stood at the down end of the up through platform: it closed in May 1959.

A half-mile of level track precedes a near mile climbing at 1 in 146 with Chislehurst station standing on embankment about midway at 11¼ miles from Charing Cross. The Kyd Brook flows to the east of the line on approach before passing beneath the up end of the platforms of the station which opened with the extension to Sevenoaks on 2nd March 1868. The station building is a replica of that at Elmstead Woods and is at the south end, also on the down side: the platforms are in the same configuration too though here they are joined by a subway. As at Elmstead Woods also the up fast platform is now devoid of buildings and canopy.

Chislehurst had substantial goods facilities where the original temporary terminus, opened on 1st July 1865 as Chislehurst & Bickley Park, had been located on the up side north of the present station. A yard of six sidings featured a large goods shed straddling one and a long row of coal bins beside another. Side and end loading were also available.

Another loading bank behind the station's up fast platform was served by a trailing connection. The down side featured a loading bank behind the down slow platform and a long refuge siding, both at the up end. The siding to the loading bank had a headshunt and was accessible by trailing connections from both the up and down slow lines. This facility had to be squeezed into a restricted space necessitating a scissors crossover to get both connections in. All goods facilities were withdrawn from 18th November 1986 though the goods shed survived for several years and two sidings in the yard were retained for some time to handle ballast traffic.

'Chislehurst Goods' signal box stood on the up side near the points into the goods yard while the main station box, a timber cabin generously fenestrated atop a tall brick locking room, was sited at the down end of the centre island platform. Both were closed on 31st May 1959 with the commissioning of the nearby 'Chislehurst Junction' panel box, located almost in the middle of the junction complex. This box also took on the working at Elmstead Woods.

Immediately beyond the station is the first of the four loops that join the SER and LCDR routes where the former crosses over the latter. These were constructed between 1902 and 1904 in conjunction with widening of the SER line after formation of the South Eastern & Chatham Railways Managing Committee in 1899. The decision had by then been taken to concentrate all Boat Train services at the LCDR's Victoria station but to continue to consider the SER's comparatively easier route to Folkestone and Dover via Orpington and Tonbridge as the main one. In part this was because the Chatham had fewer inner suburban paths to find than the South Eastern required out of London Bridge and because the Catford Loop provided a second and independent route between Brixton and Bromley.

The Down Bickley Loop, about ¾-mile long from Bickley Junction on the ex-LCDR, was opened in September 1902. It dipped down to pass beneath the South Eastern line and then climbed on a sharp reverse curve at 1 in 84 to gain the SER slow line at what became Petts Wood Junction. The corresponding Up Bickley Loop, now a little longer than its counterpart, falls on a steady 1 in 180 gradient between the two junctions from the up fast. Two more loops were opened on 19th June 1904 to permit trains to run between the South Eastern and Chatham lines. The Down Chislehurst Loop leaves the down slow just beyond the road bridge over Chislehurst's Summer Hill and falls for ½-mile at 1 in 190 to the level of the LCDR line at St Mary Cray Junction. The Up Chislehurst Loop, the longest of the four at just over a mile, makes a lonely excursion among the trees of Petts Wood before a slight dip is required to pass under the SER line alongside the down Bickley-Petts Wood loop. A sharp climb at 1 in 75/77 takes it to join the up fast line immediately south of Chislehurst station. All but the Down Chislehurst Loop were re-laid on new alignments in 1959 as part of the Kent Coast electrification scheme, the most severe curvature being eased or indeed straightened to increase line speed.

A further change was made in connection with the London Bridge re-signalling scheme. Morning rush hour trains up from the Kent Coast for Cannon Street, which had previously been routed via the Up Chislehurst Loop and therefore would now be on the wrong side of the layout if that continued, were passed instead through new point-work to traverse its down direction counterpart from St Mary Cray Junction to join the down slow line at Chislehurst. A new trailing crossover at the north end of the station was installed to transfer such trains on to the up line. Later still, in anticipation of Eurostar traffic, both the Bickley Loops were doubled. The down loop, which was realigned so as to surrender its track to the up loop, now shares its realignment with that of the Up Chislehurst Loop for the few yards that they both pass beneath the SER line.

All this to-ing and fro-ing is complete at Petts Wood Junction, just over 12¼ miles from Charing Cross. The gradient for the last mile has been at a comparatively reasonable 1 in 234 which continues through Petts Wood station (12m 53ch). The high quality estate to the east of the line and butting up to the southern border of the wood itself, which is owned and managed by the National Trust, was built during the 1920s. It is quoted as being a very fine example, indeed a classic example, of town planning of the period. The station opened on 9th July 1928 in response to this development, immediately causing much land on the west side of the line to be quickly bought up and covered with hundreds of very typical 1930s suburban semi-detached properties as well as the laying out of a street of attractive shops running close to and parallel with the railway.

The station itself consists of two island platforms, one serving the slow lines, the other the fast ones with very typical Southern Railway buildings and canopies of the period (though recently updated). The large, modern, timber booking office is on the down side at first floor level above shops and offices and leads out on to the recently-renewed footbridge providing access to the platforms as well as permitting pedestrians to cross the line. The goods yard was on the down side adjacent to the station. It consisted of three

sidings with a headshunt and a trailing connection into the down slow line. There was no goods shed here but the inevitable and very necessary coal bins lined one siding. The yard closed in October 1968 and the site now serves as a car park for the station and an adjacent supermarket.

The climb is interrupted by a short level section where there are east-to-west single-lead crossovers between all four lines, before resuming at 1 in 310 for the next 1¼ miles. Orpington, for many years now the outer limit of suburban working and where the four tracks that have been with us since New Cross become two, stands on this climb 13¾ miles from Charing Cross. A loco depot was located on the down side immediately before the station. It had been authorised in 1901, the loops at Chislehurst then under construction providing the means for LCDR-line suburban services that terminated at Bickley to be extended to Orpington. This permitted the old and rather cramped Bickley loco shed to be closed as well as much reducing light engine movements to and from the SER Bricklayers Arms depot. The allocation at its height amounted to around twenty engines. As might be expected it consisted mainly of tank locomotives of both SER and LCDR parentage and Wainwright's 'H' class. The brick-built shed had a slated pitched roof with a vent along its ridge and two dead-end roads passing through it. A 55' turntable and a coal stage were provided as well as two further sidings, and release roads to headshunts both north and south of the shed. The depot did not last long, closing upon electrification in 1926, the turntable being moved to replace the 45' one in the semi-roundhouse at Horsham. The building, however, remains in use, modified as staff quarters and offices for the extensive carriage sidings here. The loco yard area was re-laid to provide carriage berthing with a shed of five roads and a washer.

The goods yard with a long headshunt occupied a site on the opposite side of the northern approach. It consisted of three sidings with the goods shed straddling the one nearest the station forecourt. Four more sidings slightly further north permitted some marshalling to take place though one finished alongside a loading bank and cattle pens. These sidings were later electrified for stock berthing purposes. Goods facilities were withdrawn on 7th October 1968 and the whole area is now used for station car parking.

From the widening of the line completed in 1905 Orpington station had three platforms, the centre one as usual being an island though both the outer platforms had bays at the northern end, making six platform faces in all. A loading bank was squeezed into the southern end of the down slow platform with a siding that trailed into the local line before it lost its independence on merging with the fast lines south of the station. Platforms are joined by a subway though access for disabled travellers has been much improved with the completion in 2008 of a new bridge with lifts.

Brick-built entrances with booking offices are available on both sides of the line, the one on the east side being close to a bus station laid out on former railway land behind the loco shed and providing a very comprehensive service to the local area. Two more terminal platforms capable of holding twelve coaches of 'Networker' stock were added on the east side of the station in the late-1990s on the site of three berthing sidings. This keeps all suburban services for both Charing Cross and Victoria on the 'local' side of the station. Four berthing sidings for the 'Networkers' were laid down north of these platforms, the carriage shed, which had been erected at electrification over four berthing sidings already in place, being demolished to enable running lines and connecting pointwork for the new platforms to be installed and longer sidings to be laid in. At about that time the two lines through the slow platforms were signalled for bi-directional working which in practice means either can be used for terminating down local trains, a facility also now available at the down fast platform.

Two signalboxes governed movements after the 1905 widening. The north box, later 'A', straddled the goods yard headshunt, a very typical SECR timber cabin standing on a steel girder frame supported by brick piers, while the south, 'B', box was located on the end of the island platform. Both were closed when a new panel box at the up end of the centre platform was commissioned on 4th March 1962. The responsibilities of that box have since been taken by the Ashford Control Centre. Immediately south of Orpington the slow and fast lines merge by way of a double junction and the climb sharpens again to 1 in 120. The major earthwork here is a very high embankment needed to take the line over a deep dry valley that may once have contained a feeder to the north-flowing River Cray about ¾ mile to the east.

The simple two-platform station at Chelsfield, which opened with the line, is 15¼ miles into the journey. Its position made it a favoured spot with photographers in steam days because, at the up end, a high, arched bridge crossing the line together with the steep-sided chalk cutting on the down side makes a splendid frame to picture hardworking locomotives near the end of the long climb from New Cross. A refuge siding on the level behind the down platform was startlingly illustrative of the steepness of the gradient here. In true SER fashion the platforms were staggered with the footbridge just meeting the northern end of the down one though lengthening has now brought them opposite one another. The timber station building was on the up side but burned down in 1973. Its replacement could not be more different, a tall, steel-framed glass box of no character whatever and completely out of keeping with its setting.

The goods yard, of two sidings with a short headshunt, was at the south end of the station on the up side with a trailing connection into the up line. One of the sidings was tucked in behind the platform and provided side loading. The signalbox stood off the south end of the down platform opposite a trailing crossover between up and down lines and close to the yard access but this also suffered its fate by fire, in 1971. Chelsfield village itself is a mile to the east but since electrification of the line in 1935 the area west and

north of the station has been intensively developed until it is virtually contiguous with Orpington. Land to the south and east of the station is in the London Green Belt and so remains beyond the clutches of developers.

Shortly beyond station limits the cutting deepens as it leads into the 597 yards of Chelsfield tunnel, driven through the chalk and gradually curving toward the east. At the tunnel's exit the line emerges into another deep cutting though the gradient eases slightly to 1 in 170 for the last ¾-mile to the summit.

Knockholt – opened on 1st May 1876 as Halstead for Knockholt ('Alight here for Badgers Mount') - stands at 16½ miles from Charing Cross though a signalbox was provided here from the outset. This station is crammed tightly into a small gap in the flank of the chalk though the cutting side towers over the down platform. Its present name was bestowed in October 1900 though in truth it is distantly and not at all conveniently sited for either place, Halstead being over a mile away as the crow flies and Knockholt about 2½ miles and both rather further than that by road.

This is another simple station, the single-storey SER timber building – crowned by some majestically tall brick chimneys - being on the up side with a lattice footbridge to the down platform close to it. A 'cottage'-style brick building replaced it in the early-1990s, a new concrete footbridge having been installed some years beforehand. The signalbox was on the north end of the down platform beside points trailing into the down line from a refuge siding. Another siding was taken off that following purchase of land in 1898 for quarrying the chalk. After many years out of use the quarry was reopened to provide material for sea defence following the severe flooding of the North Kent coast at Reculver in 1953. Neither siding survives.

The goods yard, of two long sidings with a headshunt and, unusually for the line, a crane of 5 tons capacity, was also at the up end and accessed by a trailing point in the up line. It closed in May 1964. The north end of the station is now spanned by the reinforced concrete bridge carrying the dual carriageway A21 London-Hastings Road at another of those suggestively-named rural Kentish villages, Pratts Bottom.

Beyond Knockholt the line is once more hemmed in by a deepening chalk cutting curving gently toward the south, the summit of the climb from St Johns, to the great relief of enginemen in steam days, being at 16 miles and 70 chains from Charing Cross. The fall commences immediately at 1 in 143 and at 17¼ miles the line enters the 1 mile and 851 yards of Polhill tunnel. Its course can be followed on the surface, for at least five brick ventilation shafts stand incongruously isolated in open fields or woodland.

The scarp slope of the Downs is naturally much steeper than the dip so the cutting at the south end of the tunnel is relatively short. The M25 motorway crosses the line ten chains beyond the tunnel's south portal. Polhill Intermediate Box, closed in March 1963, stood at the point

An example of the once-regular late-summer traffic is hauled by one of Maunsell's splendid 'L1' class 4-4-0s, No 31758. This hop-pickers' 'special', formed of a six-coach set of SECR stock and very possibly bound for Paddock Wood, is seen passing Petts Wood Junction. 22 September 1956.   *R C Riley / The Transport Treasury*

where the cutting gives way to a high embankment as the line dives down the western side of the Darent valley into another short cutting and beneath the M26 motorway to reach Dunton Green. This station is just over 20½ miles from Charing Cross and opened with the line as Dunton Green & Riverhead. It became a junction in July 1881 when a four-and-a-quarter-mile long single-track branch opened from Westerham. This came in on a north facing junction, taking over the trackbed of the goods yard's single siding which trailed into the up line, the station's up platform being reconfigured into a 'V' to accommodate it. The local promoters of the branch had high hopes for its extension westward to Oxted but this never materialised. Other than in the earliest days there were only ever sporadic attempts to run through London-Westerham services. The branch was worked for many years by a push-pull shuttle diagrammed for Tonbridge engines and crews though runround loops were provided at both ends for freight traffic and the occasional excursion. Nor did the branch figure in the Kent Coast Electrification Scheme: it closed on 30th October 1961.

The Westerham Valley Railway Association made heroic efforts to save the line for preservation but Government had already earmarked much of the route for use by part of the southern section of the new M25 London Orbital motorway. Evidence remains at Dunton Green where some of the trackbed westward to the A21 Sevenoaks by-pass is now a public footpath. To those who do not know the history the reason for the seemingly unnecessary hump-backed bridge by which the branch passed under the London Road is surely a mystery, especially as residential development and landscaping have much reduced the clearance beneath and around it.

Dunton Green station now consists only of up and down platforms joined by a footbridge with the timber station building, again featuring tall brick chimneys, on the up side. A public subway passes underneath the station. The goods yard, of three closely-spaced sidings, was taken off the down end of the branch's platform line: it closed in April 1962.

When the Westerham branch opened the signalbox, a timber building on a tall and narrow brick locking room, was relocated into the 'V' of the converging lines. But prior to Grouping in 1923 it was shifted again, to the northern end

Bulleid 'light' Pacific, No 34021 'Dartmoor', winds its careful way alongside Platform 3 at London bridge with the down 'Man of Kent', the 1.10 pm departure from Charing Cross. Its ultimate destination is Margate, travelling by way of Folkestone, Dover, Deal and Ramsgate. 14 May 1959.　　　　　　　　　　　　　　　　*R C Riley / The Transport Treasury*

of the down platform. An aerial ropeway was constructed from it across the main lines to a small platform reached by a ramped walkway so that the single line tablet could be collected or delivered by the crew of the branch engine. This rather unsatisfactory arrangement lasted until September 1934 when the token machine was moved to a room on the up platform. South of the station, on the down side, a private siding led into the works of the Dunton Green Brick & Tile Company, further evidence of the clay subsoil in the area. The works closed in 1965.

The line makes a curving climb out of the Darent Valley at 1 in 160 for two miles, bridging the river in the process. Sevenoaks is near the head of the climb at 22 miles and 9 chains into the journey. Much of Sevenoaks itself is south and east of the station and standing well above its level on the greensand ridge through which the line subsequently tunnels. It developed around the junction of two major roads, nowadays the A224 but originally the London Road, later turnpiked, and the A225 from the Thames at Dartford, though there had been a settlement here before the town was granted 'Market' status in the 13th century. Housing

development that followed the coming of the railway has crept further and further down the hill until Edwardian villas and later 'infills' have now reached its foot.

The station opened officially on 2nd March 1868 and to the public the next day with the line from Chislehurst. The suffix 'Tub's Hill' – the road on which it stands - was added on 1st August 1869 when the Sevenoaks Railway (opened 2nd June 1862 and worked from Swanley by the LCDR) extended its line there from the town's Bat & Ball station a mile to the north east. Four through lines were provided from opening, the easternmost one having a platform on each side: south-facing bay platforms were later added on both sides of the station. The eastern bay had a runround loop reached by a turntable at its northern end. This arrangement lasted well into the 1940s despite the steam-powered Sevenoaks-Tonbridge locals being worked push/pull for many years. But a radical upgrade preceded the arrival of Eurostar trains when some realignment and straightening and usage of track through the station, which included the later abolition of both bay platforms, was complemented by re-signalling all but the up main for reversible working. (South of Sevenoaks the line continues to be signalled for bi-directional working until the immediate approach to Tonbridge.)

Two timber signalboxes governed movements, one being in the 'V' of the converging line from Bat & Ball, the other on the up side at the south end of the station. They were originally identified as 'no. 1' and 'no. 2' but after nationalisation were re-designated 'A' and 'B'. Closure came on 4th March 1962 when the Chislehurst-Hildenborough section was re-signalled in connection with phase 2 of the Kent Coast Electrification scheme. The area has since come under the control of the Ashford signalling centre.

The station now has two island platforms and a bland steel and glass building on a bridge spanning the tracks. It was the first built under the Network SouthEast red, white and blue banner, superseding the original timber structure on the down side.

The goods yard was sited on the up side. For a town the size of Sevenoaks – c11,000 in 1931 – it was relatively small with only four sidings, one of which was very short. Two were lined by coal bins while the goods shed straddled the third. Two more short sidings with a headshunt were added later on the down side of the incoming line from Bat & Ball. A loading bank stood between these with cattle pens on one side in close proximity to the cattle market at the foot of Tubs Hill. The yard closed in October 1972 and now forms the station car park though a single siding remains in place. (It may be noted that there were also goods facilities at Bat & Ball station consisting of a goods shed, cattle pens and coal yard.)

To the south of the station there were several sidings, two quite lengthy ones on the up side being classified as 'Up Quarry Sidings'. Opposite these were two carriage sidings, later electrified though only one remains now. However, it is configured by facing points off the down line to be classified as two in tandem capable of holding eight- and twelve-coach trains respectively. The quarry sidings have also been lifted though the trackbed of the one nearest the up line was used to extend the up loop on its change to 'up fast' for Eurostar traffic.

The summit of the climb from Dunton Green lies at 22½ miles: thirteen chains further on is the northern portal of Sevenoaks tunnel where the gradient is already falling at 1 in 144 for the whole of the tunnel's 1 mile 1693 yards. The first few chains are on a slight curve, turning the line to face more toward the south. At the tunnel exit the gradient steepens to 1 in 122 and a half mile beyond it Weald Intermediate Box once stood on the up side to break the long section to Hildenborough. A siding available for public use trailed into the up line right beside it.

The station at Hildenborough, which lends its name to the 6-mile long bank between Sevenoaks and Tonbridge, is approached in a deep cutting which is bridged at its northern end by the dual carriageway A21 Hastings Road. It opened with the line but stands some way to the west of the village at 27 miles from Charing Cross. The up side buildings, which have twice been refurbished in recent years, are in the, by now, usual lapped timber though the road side is now rendered. A lattice footbridge joins the two platforms, the down one having a short refuge siding behind it. The goods yard, which opened four years after the station itself, consisted of two sidings on the up side, the headshunt being accessible from both up and down lines. It closed in October 1960 and the signalbox, located at the south end of the up platform, followed on 4th March 1962.

The line continues to plunge downgrade, in cutting for the next mile or so, before briefly touching ambient ground level and then continuing on embankment to reach and level out across the flood plain of the River Medway. The line curves to face almost due south again on approach to the river bridge (28m 76ch), following which is the sharp 90° curve that takes it to Tonbridge West Junction, 29 miles and 35 chains from Charing Cross. The original line of the approach curve was severe enough to warrant a 20mph speed restriction though it was eased out to 22 chains radius in 1935 as part of the station's rebuilding. This still necessitated a speed restriction but raised to 40mph for down trains and 50 mph for those in the up direction. Further easing took place at electrification in 1962 though speed restrictions still apply.

Tonbridge station lies seven chains further on and is built in the style the South Eastern adopted for its major junctions, with the platforms served by loops off the main lines. Up end bays were provided on both platforms though the up side one was made a through road by the Southern in 1935 as part of the station's upgrading. All five lines through the station are now signalled for reversible working with the exception of the up fast. Since privatisation the station building, on the bridge over the line at the down end, and those on the platforms, have been refurbished and upgraded.

The South Eastern designed the brick building to make a statement about the importance the railway attached to itself and to the town, being very large and quite grandiose, particularly for a structure placed on a bridge. In consequence the bridge itself has been constructed on a matching scale, each of the four through lines passing under an individual arch. The Southern merely provided a plain girder span when making the up side bay into a loop: it bears only the weight of the road. The 1935 upgrade of the building was particularly unsympathetic, for the tops of the round-headed windows were lowered and squared off and the characteristically-patterned brickwork rendered. It has to be said the most recent 'improvements' to it, the road side now faced with brown and mustard coloured tiles, could also be described as a contradiction in terms!

Two signalboxes governed movements in and around the station. These were both on the down side, one right by the West Junction, the other straddling the down slow line at the East Junction where the Hastings line curved away south. This box had been rebuilt and re-equipped in

1934. They lasted until 18th March 1962 when the Hildenborough-Paddock Wood/High Brooms section of the Kent Coast re-signalling scheme was commissioned and a new panel box opened in the 'V' of the west junction. Ashford now exercises control.

Three banks of sidings were laid down in 1941 on the down side of the line from Redhill because the Hoo Junction sidings, lying open and exposed on the marshes between Gravesend and Higham, had been identified as particularly vulnerable to air attack. In the event of their becoming unusable Tonbridge yard could be brought into action. The fact is the volume of traffic being handled necessitated both yards working almost constantly. The sidings nowadays are used only for berthing and crew changing purposes. The goods yard itself was separated either side of the line east of the station, most facilities being to the north with the coal yard on the up side of the incoming Hastings line.

"Tonbridge Loco" was in the 'V' of the Hastings line convergence and had been established with the arrival of the Redhill line in 1842. Its allocation was at its height in the 1930s when some fifty engines were on the books but this number steadily declined after the 1935 electrification from Orpington to Sevenoaks until only ten were left in 1962. Classified 74D and later 73J by BR, the shed closed in June 1964.

The line has suffered four fatal accidents, three of them involving passenger trains with serious loss of life. On 7th June 1884 a double-headed freight train ran into the back of another in Sevenoaks station: the crew of the leading engine were killed. The South Eastern has to be given credit for being among the first to adopt the Block system, the main line having been equipped throughout by the end of 1852. But being a pioneer has its drawbacks and the early instrumentation still in use here, a single block instrument for both lines, caused some confusion between the Hildenborough signalman and his colleague at Sevenoaks. The Inspecting officer came to the conclusion the former was chiefly to blame: he was subsequently charged with manslaughter.

The first of the trio of passenger train disasters occurred less than three miles to the north. On 24th August 1927 Maunsell 'River' class 2-6-4T engine no. 800, *River Cray*, left Cannon Street with the 5.00pm express for Dover and Deal. In the deep chalk cutting about 250 yards beyond the south portal of Polhill tunnel the leading driving wheels mounted the rail and dropped over to the nearside. Another 200 yards or so further on the engine had slewed far enough out of gauge for the cab to strike the centre pier of a bridge spanning the cutting. Completely derailed now, *River Cray* slewed still further before coming heavily to rest on its side leaning against the cutting wall with the leading coaches piled up against it. There were thirteen fatalities and twenty serious injuries and much damage to stock. Three new Maunsell coaches were broken up on the spot as well as the Pullman car 'Carmen'. This finished up almost sideways

across the track, its weight and that of the following vehicles having crushed and virtually reduced to matchwood the coach preceding it which had become wedged against the bridge piers.

This was not the first derailment of a 'River' though the previous ones, also of the leading drivers or the Bissel truck, had fortunately not had serious consequences. Tests made during the subsequent enquiry by Col. Sir John Pringle showed the engines to be 'track sensitive' rather than defective in basic design though water surging about in the side tanks was held to be a probable factor in the problem. On the Great Northern line out of Kings Cross, with Nigel Gresley on the footplate, the sole 3-cylinder representative of the class, the K1 no. 890, rode admirably at speeds up to 83¼ mph though noted as being 'lively on the springs'. Yet even on South Western track out of Waterloo, with its good Meldon granite ballast, again with Gresley observing, the riding of the engines tested was described as varying between 'uncomfortable' and 'unsafe', being characterised by sudden lurches and violent rolling. All twenty-one were withdrawn and rebuilt, to return nameless as 2-6-0 tender locomotives. Also as a result of the accident the Dungeness shingle ballast still in use on this line was quickly removed in favour of Meldon granite on the orders of the Southern's General Manager, the estimable Sir Herbert Walker. One man deeply affected by the smash was the Chief Engineer, George Ellson, who had been with the SECR before Grouping and on whose former 'patch' it occurred. He scuppered Maunsell's planned 2-6-2 mixed traffic engine of 1934 on the basis of the overall weight, and questioned the use of a leading pony truck on so heavy an engine. He also placed an embargo on the later 'W' class 2-6-4 tank engines hauling passenger trains, though they regularly worked empty stock.

The second of this trio occurred in the heavy fog blanketing South London on 4th December 1957. The weather conditions had so disrupted the timetable that the 4.56pm Folkestone and Ramsgate express left Cannon Street behind 'Battle of Britain' class 4-6-2 no. 34066 *Spitfire* sixty-eight minutes late. Ironically this was the same train as had been involved at Dunton Green thirty years earlier but slightly retimed following the fire in Cannon Street signalbox on 5th April that year. (The new box was commissioned on 15th December.) Despite the fog the powerful beams of the 4-aspect colour-light signals were relatively easy to pick out at distance. But for clearance reasons the signals in the cutting between New Cross and St Johns were placed on the right-hand side of the track. In normal circumstances the slight left-hand curvature of this section would have made the first two visible to the driver from his usual position on the left-hand side of the footplate, even beyond the long boiler casing. The fog, however, made his sighting them impossible. As was his custom the fireman, on passing New Cross, had begun to build up the fire for the long climb to Knockholt and did not therefore see these two signals which were respectively displaying double-yellow and single-yellow aspects. The driver, William Trew of Ramsgate shed, a very experienced man, did not ask him to do so nor did he cross the footplate himself to spot them. He could give no reason subsequently for this lapse beyond saying that he had never been checked at them before.

At the approach to St Johns the fireman momentarily ceased work to check the Home signal because the driver could not have seen it as the curve straightened out. He immediately called to Trew, "You've got a red!" The driver made a full emergency brake application but the train was travelling at about 40mph and there was no hope of pulling up at the signal. Not far beyond it the ten-coach 5.18pm Charing Cross-Hayes train was standing with brakes fully applied on the gradient at Parks Bridge Junction because the signalman there was uncertain exactly which train it was. *Spitfire* crashed into its rear at an estimated 34mph, telescoping the ninth coach right through the body of the eighth. Unfortunately the collision occurred almost beneath the girder bridge carrying the Nunhead-Lewisham line. Though the engine held the rails its tender was thrown to the left, dislodging a supporting column and bringing the 350-ton truss girder and bridge deck crashing down on to the leading coach of the Ramsgate train and the front part of the second one. Ninety people lost their lives in this disaster and 109 were seriously injured. This figure might have been worse but for the prompt action of the driver of the 5.22pm Holborn Viaduct-Dartford service who saw the fallen bridge dipping away from him in the darkness as he slowly approached it, and stopped his train on the brink.

This was the third worst rail accident in Britain and came only five years after the second worst, the double collision at Harrow & Wealdstone. The bridge was temporarily rebuilt with a military trestle which is still in service, a mute though salutary reminder of driver Trew's sad lapse. However, while not in the least condoning or excusing Trew's actions, but knowing other circumstances, it is impossible not to feel some sympathy for him. He had already been on duty for more than six hours, having brought a train up from the coast earlier in the day. Now, quite apart from the problems posed to them by the fog, he and his fireman must have got very cold and frustrated while waiting for well over an hour on the platform end at Cannon Street before the empty stock of the train finally drew in from Rotherhithe Sidings. As was customary in many such workings *Spitfire*, which had travelled to Rotherhithe during the afternoon 'light' from Stewarts Lane, was already attached at the head. But the long delay in getting to Cannon Street had much depleted the water supply in the tender. This so concerned Trew that he had told the guard and the station staff he would have to call specially at Sevenoaks to replenish it. The fact the line falls from just beyond that station and the engine could therefore have coasted under minimum steaming all the way to the train's first scheduled stop at Tonbridge is the strongest indication of that concern. No doubt this problem in particular much preoccupied him and there is a suggestion that even this early in the journey he may already have been 'nursing' the engine because of it.

Driver Trew was subsequently tried for the manslaughter of the guard of the Hayes train but the jury could not reach a verdict. A planned retrial was dropped when the prosecution said no evidence would be offered because of his deteriorating mental and physical condition. It is not too strong a point to make that William Trew became in time another victim of the Lewisham disaster.

This sombre trio was completed ten years later and only two miles away. That Sunday evening in the late-autumn of 1967 was far from quiet for it happened to be 5th November. The 19.43 Hastings-Charing Cross train consisted of two of the 6-car diesel-electric units introduced to the line in 1957, nos. 1007 and 1017. They were travelling on the up fast line at about 70mph when, a mile north of Grove Park station, the offside leading wheel of the third coach struck a small wedge-shaped piece that had broken away from the end of a rail. The wheels were derailed to the off side and about a ¼-mile further on struck the lead of a diamond crossover in the up fast line. This caused all the coaches from the second to the twelfth to become completely derailed. The second, third, fourth and fifth coaches turned over on to their sides and continued travelling in this fashion for some distance before coming to rest strewn across both up and down through lines and an adjacent reception road for the up yard.

The coupling broke behind the first coach, which was not derailed, severance of the brake hoses bringing it to a stand some 250 yards ahead of the rest of its train and about 750 yards south of Hither Green station. There were forty-nine fatalities and seventy-eight people injured, twenty-seven seriously.

The Inspector, Col. McMullen, concluded that the direct cause lay at the rail end where a cracked concrete sleeper had been replaced by a timber one of shallower section without adequate packing support beneath it, evidenced by pumping conditions. This lack of good support had stressed the fishplate and rail end causing fatigue fractures which spread from around the bolt holes and in time resulted in the separation of the wedge from the rail end, almost certainly as this train passed over it.

McMullen also made comments on the axle-loading of the bogies under the heavy diesel engine and generator at the outer ends of the motor coaches, most particularly in the light of the very restricted side-to-side movement of the bolster relative to the bogie frame. Such a restriction was necessary because of the tight loading gauge clearances in the tunnels south of Tonbridge. But the Inspector concluded any sudden sideways movement would impart a considerable shock to the rails when that movement was brought to an equally sudden halt. This holds especially true where the bogie hits a low joint which causes it to turn rapidly into and out of the dip. Track and trackbed maintenance in general over this part of the route came in for some harsh criticism. The Colonel also noted that the 70mph speed limit was not always adhered to though the questioned operations officer who admitted this said that the proportion of speeding trains was small as was the excess itself. (From personal experience of daily travel to and from North Kent in that period I can confirm that this appeared to be a tempting section on which to make up any lost time if the road was clear. The riding was always, shall we say, lively!) Like the Hastings diesels, diamond crossings no longer bedevil this part of the route but there are still a considerable number of crossovers in the 1¾ miles between Grove Park and Hither Green demanding first-class maintenance.

To turn to more cheerful things: O S Nock noted a number of runs over the route timed by J Pearson Pattinson during the last few years of the South Eastern's independence and later published. No exact speeds at timing points appear to have been recorded but the averages are still illuminating. All the trips were made behind Stirling 'F' class engines hauling gross loads varying between 160 and 280 tons. These engines had a relatively small boiler of 985 sq ft pressed at 160 psi with a grate area of only 16½ sq ft but it had to feed large 19" x 26" cylinders. The performances suggest the boiler must have been an excellent steamer.

Even after the turn of the 19th century, South Eastern trains were nominally restricted to a maximum of 60mph yet these express engines were fitted with wheels no less than 7' 0" in diameter. It is possible the company's Engineer, Francis Brady, set the speed limit knowing that, despite the neat and tidy appearance SER track always presented, the shingle Dungeness ballast beneath and around it was difficult to compact really adequately to provide good support to and alignment of the track. Knowing Watkin however it is quite probable he insisted on this limit to reduce the drain on the Track Renewals Account as well as on loco maintenance costs. Whichever may be the case, the Stirling classes, even before rebuilding with Wainwright boilers, were shown to be perfectly capable of travelling rather faster than that. No. 240 went to the Paris exhibition of 1889 and subsequently made some runs on the PLM in which she quite happily reached speeds in excess of 70mph with a maximum of 79mph. Be that as it may locomotive work over the 'Cut-off' was generally of a very high standard.

One fairly consistent fact thrown up by these records is that the timings and average speeds frequently achieved either side of Tonbridge, particularly in the down direction, indicate a very liberal view was often taken of the 20mph speed limit on the curve at Tonbridge West Junction. Indeed, on occasions trains appear to have gone round it on the proverbial 'one wheel'.

The published runs show very competent work across the board over the 11¾ miles between New Cross and Knockholt (Halstead). For example, no. 210 with a load of 170 tons averaged 35.8 mph while no. 156, faced with 280 tons, completed the climb at an outstanding 32.8mph. This compares very favourably with an average of 32.2 mph put up by no. 130 hauling 230 tons. (On that run incidentally - if the timings are correct! - the average on the near two miles between Dunton Green and Sevenoaks, uphill at 1 in 160, was no less than 61.7mph!) Although running across The

Weald was always quite restrained, even in the light of the 60mph maximum, the respective averages of 53, 52.3 and 52.7 mph for the subsequent 5¼ miles to Paddock Wood would suggest the permanent restriction at Tonbridge West Junction was shown short shrift on all three runs.

No. 160, heading a Hastings train of 160 tons gross, suffered a severe signal check before Grove Park but recovered brilliantly on the easier grades south of Chislehurst to average over 40mph from there to Orpington and complete the climb from New Cross to Halstead in twenty-one minutes exactly, an excellent average of 33.6mph, signal check notwithstanding.

No. 130 features again in two runs made on up services from Margate via Canterbury (now West). These tended to have sharper timings than the Folkestone expresses because of fiercer competition with the LCDR which had the shorter route. The thirteen miles up from Tonbridge to Halstead have a breather in the form of the two downhill miles from the north end of Sevenoaks tunnel. But the speed restriction at Tonbridge West Junction should not have permitted a run to be taken at the opening uphill six miles though, once again, records suggest a very liberal interpretation of it for that purpose.

With a load of 160 tons no. 130 took just 11m 16s for the 7½ miles from Tonbridge to Sevenoaks, an average of all but 40mph while a heavier load of 220 tons was taken through in 12m 40s at a very commendable 35.5mph. The four miles from Dunton Green up to Halstead were covered at 39.8 and 39.7mph respectively despite the speed at the start, in both cases, apparently being well below the maximum permitted 60mph. These examples are given as representative of the general level of work attained over the line at the time. Other than the signal check noted above with no. 160 all trains had a clear run throughout and when, be it remarked, there were still only two tracks north of Orpington, which says a lot about the generally high standard of South Eastern operating then.

Nock also records some runs timed by the experienced - if not always reliable! - Charles Rous-Marten made after the 'working arrangement' of 1899. Two up direction services feature Stirling's later 'B' class 4-4-0 alongside Wainwright's splendid class 'D' 4-4-0, surely among the most visually satisfying locomotive classes ever to emerge from a British railway workshop. The 'Folkestone Pullman Car' train, weighing 200 tons behind the tender, was allowed 90 minutes for its non-stop run of 68.7 miles from Folkestone Central to Cannon Street. The 'B' was in all mechanical respects similar to the earlier 'F' class but the boiler had a slightly greater heating surface and grate area was a little larger. By contrast the 'D', an altogether bigger engine, had a boiler pressed at 175psi and a tractive effort of 17,453 lbs against the 15,200 of the 'B'. Nevertheless the smaller engine, no. 453, more than held her own, for she averaged 34 mph from Tonbridge to the north end of Sevenoaks tunnel against the 33.3 mph of the 'D', no. 745. She also had the edge on the climb from Dunton Green,

'C' class 0-6-0 No 31694 takes the sharply curved last few yards of the Dartford Loop as it approaches Hither Green from Lee Loop Junction with an up freight. 2 May 1959.   *R C Riley / The Transport Treasury*

averaging 44.4mph to Knockholt whereas no. 745 averaged 43.6mph. Despite permanent way slacks and signal checks further on both arrived comfortably before the scheduled time.

In the down direction 'D' no. 734 had charge of the non-stop 4.36pm Cannon Street-Folkestone business train loaded to 250 tons. The start was hampered by permanent way slacks after Grove Park and before Chislehurst but the engine still averaged over 36mph from the Chislehurst slack to passing Knockholt. Combined with a further slack before Sevenoaks the train was nearly four minutes behind time at Tonbridge. As seemed to be the way however, running across The Weald was quite pedestrian, even given the generally rising nature of the 26.6 miles to Ashford where three vehicles were slipped. But there followed quite brilliant work on the long climb to Westenhanger, the 8.1 miles being run in only 8¾ minutes, an average of 55½ mph. That and a brisk finish brought the train into Folkestone a little less than two minutes late in a net time of 83 minutes.

That doyen of recorders, Cecil J Allan, also published a number of runs over the route with Wainwright's

later 'E' class and their rebuilds. 'E' no. 176 was tackling a load of 325 tons when hauling the important 9.5pm Folkestone Harbour-Charing Cross boat train. The run had been going to time until the approach to Tonbridge where signal checks, including a momentary dead stand to the east of the station, were so severe as to make the train ten minutes late. From this standing start no. 176 had reached 25½mph up the long grind to Hildenborough and entered Sevenoaks tunnel at 28mph. By the exit, despite the easing of the grade within, speed had fallen slightly to 26½mph. Sevenoaks tunnel is wet and the drop may well have been due to slipping or the driver easing the regulator to prevent it. By contrast no. 179, with the 320-ton 7.55pm up from Dover Pier, which had also been checked at Tonbridge though not nearly as seriously, actually accelerated from 28mph at the tunnel's entrance to 30mph at the exit. Knockholt was passed at 35mph and 33mph respectively. These performances reflect excellent work with such heavy loads.

CJA also provided further logs of runs made after all Continental traffic had been switched to Victoria. 'E' class no. 115 was recorded not long before the grouping with an up Dover boat train timed to take 110 minutes. This timing is evidently very generous but it is clear from the schedule slow running was still being imposed through Folkestone Warren following stabilisation work on the great landslip of 1915. The load is quoted as 315 tons and there is not a single signal check over the whole of the 78 miles of the journey. Regrettably only average speeds are noted and no timings were taken at the ends of Sevenoaks tunnel. Tonbridge was passed 1m 40s early but this had been whittled away to a mere five seconds by Sevenoaks. Nevertheless the 6.4 mainly uphill miles were covered at an average speed of 24¾ mph. It is clear the curve at Tonbridge was shown rather greater respect than appears to have been the case on the earlier runs. Relatively easy running is also evident on the climb to Knockholt for nearly a minute was dropped over the section from Dunton Green. But Beckenham Junction was passed on time, and an early arrival would have been quite possible but for a PWS at Sydenham Hill. The net time was calculated at 106½ minutes.

A down boat train, also of 315 tons gross, was headed by the Maunsell-rebuilt 'E1' class no. 497. Bickley Junction was passed only a few seconds late but this had changed to nearly two minutes early at Knockholt, only five miles further on: speed there was 32½mph. Nothing higher than 60mph was noted passing Dunton Green but the train was still 1¼ minutes early at Sevenoaks. Tonbridge West curve was taken at 20mph precisely, ¾ minute ahead of schedule and despite a PWS before Dover, arrival was still ½ minute early, the net time being 96 minutes. Again, no signal checks were experienced but the engine was clearly absolute master of the job and the unchecked run reflects the driver's pretty close adherence to the working timetable, the sort of performance much appreciated by the Operating Department! Without doubt the 'E1' was one of the all-time classics of locomotive design. It is the greatest pity none survived the breaker's torch.

Finally, a run with one of the last class designed by Wainwright, the 'L' 4-4-0. Maunsell inherited the drawings in which some retrograde alterations appear subsequently to have made to the valve settings. The class in general found it difficult to keep time consistently with the 80-minute Folkestone expresses to which they were allocated when new, particularly in making up any time lost due to out-of-course delays. But they were found to be ideal for the demanding Hastings line which played to their strengths but covered their weaknesses.

Allen timed no. 765 as far as its stop at Crowhurst with the 3.40pm Charing Cross to Hastings, a train of 235 tons. Signal checks put it 2½ minutes late as early as London Bridge but then a clear road was enjoyed throughout. Another ¼ minute had been dropped by Hither Green but recovery started in earnest from there. Orpington was passed two minutes down at 49mph and a further ½ minute had been recovered at Knockholt where the speed had fallen away only to 43mph. Another ½ minute had been regained by Sevenoaks although Dunton Green was passed at a relatively

modest 64½mph. By Tonbridge the lateness was down to less than a minute and an excellent climb over that fearsome gradient up to High Brooms (Southborough) saw the train through Tunbridge Wells ¼ minute early.

There are nowadays no scheduled non-stop passenger workings of any description over the route since Channel Tunnel traffic was switched to the high-speed line from St Pancras. The franchise is presently held by 'southeastern' which has class 375 units for main line services and classes 465 and 466 together with the newer class 376 sets – a breakaway from Southern tradition in that each set is five coaches long – for suburban work.

Off-peak Orpington attracts eight trains each hour from/to London Bridge which, since privatisation, has seen a marked rise in its own fortunes: no longer do fast trains for the coast make Waterloo East their last London call. Of these Orpington services two emanate half-hourly from Cannon Street and terminate, having served all stations via Lewisham. Two more are Charing Cross/Sevenoaks services that run fast between London Bridge and Hither Green and call at all stations south of there. In the down direction these stand at Orpington beside half-hourly Hastings trains that leave Charing Cross nine minutes later and which then run ahead of them, fast to Sevenoaks. One of these calls only at Wadhurst, Battle and St Leonards south of Tunbridge Wells, its opposite number stopping at all stations. Twice hourly Tunbridge Wells trains call, again fast from/to London Bridge: these serve Sevenoaks and all stations south. In addition four trains each hour on a fifteen-minute headway work a Victoria-Orpington via Beckenham Junction service calling at all stations *en route.*

Another recent introduction in association with First Capital Connect sees four up trains departing from quite early in the weekday morning peak to provide a through service to Kentish Town and beyond via Bromley South and Blackfriars. Though these serve St Pancras International there is, at the time of writing, no corresponding service at this level in the opposite direction.

Sevenoaks sees an equally comprehensive service. In addition to the trains noted above which call or terminate there this station enjoys a half-hourly service to/from the Kent Coast, dividing at Ashford. Of these trains one portion terminates at Dover Priory while the second portion takes the line up the Stour valley to Canterbury West with an hourly continuation to Ramsgate. Sevenoaks also has a half-hourly stopping service to/from Kentish Town. However, this is not routed through Orpington but runs via Swanley, Bromley South, the Catford Loop and Blackfriars calling at all stations to provide a direct if somewhat time-consuming connection to St Pancras International. This service has a longstanding pedigree, for many years making Holborn Viaduct its London terminus before that station closed with the re-opening of Snow Hill tunnel in 1988.

As might be expected Tonbridge retains its status as an important transport node. Off-peak in the up direction it despatches six trains each hour to Charing Cross via

Sevenoaks. Southwards there are the two trains each hour to Hastings, the two to Tunbridge Wells and the two to Dover and Canterbury West with the Canterbury portion extended hourly to Ramsgate, all as noted above. A hint of that which got the South Eastern into hot water in the first place takes the form of an hourly service to Strood via Paddock Wood and Maidstone West. In addition 'Southern' works an hourly semi-fast service between London Bridge and Redhill and all stations thence to Tonbridge, the Brighton openly retaliating perhaps! It may be remarked that all stations on the 'cut-off' now have platforms long enough to accommodate trains of twelve coaches.

What of the future? Well, while not directly concerned with the 'Cut-off' *per se,* work west of North Kent East Junction will eventually see Charing Cross services diving down the presently disused double track ramp that once lead to Rotherhithe Road carriage sidings and Bricklayers Arms loco depot, to rise on a new ramp in the vicinity of South Bermondsey station. This will permit trains off the Brighton line working the much enhanced Thameslink service to pass above them rather than crossing on the level as they do now. By this they will gain direct access to their dedicated route through London Bridge to Blackfriars Junction presently also used by Charing Cross services east of Metropolitan Junction. At London Bridge itself three terminal platforms in the Brighton part of the station will be transformed on a higher level into three through platforms for Charing Cross trains, the tracks through them leading to the new pair currently under construction across Borough Market. A revamped station concourse and improved bus interchange in the forecourt are also planned.

No doubt the opportunities presented by the ongoing Thameslink project will see further increases in services over the Sevenoaks cut-off to take advantage of available travel destinations unthinkable when the line was first proposed.

Bibliography

History of the Southern Railway, C F Dendy Marshall, Revised by R W Kidner, Ian Allan Ltd., 1963
Sir Herbert Walker's Southern Railway, C F Klapper, Ian Allan Ltd., 1973
The South Eastern & Chatham Railway, O S Nock, Ian Allan Ltd., 1961
Charing Cross to Orpington, Vic Mitchell and Keith Smith, Middleton Press, 1991
Orpington to Tonbridge, Vic Mitchell and Keith Smith, Middleton Press, 1992
Swanley to Ashford, Vic Mitchell and Keith Smith, Middleton Press, 1995
Railways of the Southern Region, Geoffrey Body, Patrick Stephens Ltd., 1984 (updated edition 1989)
An Historical Survey of Southern Sheds, Chris Hawkins and George Reeve, Oxford Publishing Co., 1979
British Railway Tunnels, Alan Blower, Ian Allan Ltd., 1964
South Eastern & Chatham Railway Album, P K Jones, Ian Allan Ltd., 1984
Red for Danger, L T C Rolt, Pan Books, 1966
Richard Maunsell, An Engineering Biography, J E Chacksfield, The Oakwood Press, 1998
Maunsell Locomotives, Brian Haresnape, Ian Allan Ltd., 1977
Allan C Baker, Letter to the Editor of 'British Railways Illustrated' magazine, March 2011
Report on the Derailment at Hither Green, HMSO, 1968
Railway Track Diagrams No 5, Southern & TfL, Gerald Jacobs, TRACKmaps, 1994 (3rd edition 2008)
TRACKatlas of Mainland Britain TRACKmaps, 2009
Jowett's Railway Atlas of Great Britain & Ireland, Alan Jowett, Guild Publishing by arrangement with Patrick Stephens, 1989
Pre-Grouping Railway Junction Diagrams 1914, Ian Allan Ltd., (undated)
British Rail Main Line Gradient Profiles, Ian Allan Ltd., (undated)
Ordnance Survey Maps 1:50000 nos 177 and 188, and Explorer 1:25000 no 162

The website moderated by the Southern Electric Group concerning the Kent Coast electrification scheme has been consulted, as have those by National Rail Enquiries, Southeastern, First Capital Connect and Southern for timetable information. I have also referred to various Wikipedia sites for confirmatory details of some of the stations en route. I am most grateful to all contributors to these sites.

'Schools' No 30923, 'Bradfield', in absolutely filthy condition, approaches New Cross with a down Folkestone and Dover train. The reporting number 133 on the smokebox probably indicates this is an 'extra; or relief working. The up side connection to the East London line may be seen just beyond the trailing crossover to the left of the train. 15 September 1957.
A E Bennett / The Transport Treasury

A "BRIT" (and others) at DOVER

Mike King

Of the twelve British Railways standard designs, probably just over half could be classed as regular sightings on the Southern Region. The Britannia pacifics could just come into this category but were always relatively uncommon. Two members of the class (Nos. 70004/14) were allocated to Stewarts Lane from 1951 until 1958 for working the Golden Arrow and other boat trains to Folkestone and Dover. One more (No. 70009) also did a stint at Nine Elms for the Bournemouth Belle and Royal Wessex in 1951 (as did 70014 briefly), but apart from special workings and the May 1953 crisis following Merchant Navy No. 35020 "Bibby Line" breaking its crank axle at Crewkerne, when seven 'Britannias' were loaned to the Region, such sightings were unusual. At the time of writing the reverse is true, as both preserved examples have been seen on specials in the southeast over recent months.

Above - *No. 70004 "William Shakespeare" arrives at Dover Marine with the down Golden Arrow on 10th May 1952 – the crew appearing well aware of the photographer's presence! At this time the train left Victoria at 11am and the picture would have been taken around 12.30pm. Later in the autumn the departure time was altered to 2pm (one hour earlier in winter), running to Folkestone Harbour instead, requiring the loco to be turned and serviced at Folkestone Junction before hauling the empty Pullmans tender-first to Dover Marine in the late afternoon, prior to the return working at times that varied somewhat from year to year - between 5.13 and 5.55pm being noted. From 1960 the down departure time of 11am was reinstated, as was the Dover destination, but by then the "Brits" had long gone. On the left an up boat train departs, with a Bulleid brake third in "blood and custard" livery at the rear. A. E West R1524*

Opposite top - *A short time later we see the loco reversing onto Dover shed prior to being turned. The immaculate turnout was typical for the "Arrow" but not regrettably for most locomotives in Kent at that time. However, the staff at Stewarts Lane were not quite finished yet... as we shall see. The loco was previously exhibited at the Festival of Britain on the South Bank and had been specially prepared for this prior to its arrival at Stewarts Lane in September 1951. A. E. West R1527*

Above - *Now turned, the loco is adjacent to the coaling plant. Alongside are N15 No.30796 "Sir Dodinas Le Savage" and a mogul – the more usual motive power at this location. With the recent special edition model of 70004 from Hornby, 4mm scale modellers could recreate this scene exactly using ready-to-run models.* A. E. West R1528

Above - Now over the ash pits we have a front-end view – showing the headboard, flags and head code discs, complete with Stewarts Lane duty no. 4 repeated on each. Additional SR lamp brackets have been bolted on to the smoke deflector support stays to give the six required SR head code positions (only needed for a boat train if diverted via Maidstone East – which could happen), but note the height above the buffer beam of the head code discs compared to later. N15 No. 30797 "Sir Blamor De Ganis" now appears alongside.   *A. E. West R1530*

Opposite top - Ready for the return working, but the immaculate finish has now been marred by either coal dust or perhaps dirty water/condensation from the ejectors at the front of the tender. The up departure was scheduled for either late afternoon or early evening (depending on GMT/BST) and the author recalls seeing this loco passing Sandling Junction one Sunday evening in the spring of 1958, not long before the two 'Britannias' were transferred away.   *A. E. West R1531*

Opposite bottom - The two Britannia's were employed on other services than the "Arrer". Here is No. 70004 at Dover again but on a rather wet 30th May 1953, being used for a pre-Coronation Day special. Notice the additional horizontal bracket across the lower smoke box, above the 73A shed plate – normally invisible behind the Golden Arrow headboard and fitted to ensure that the board sat vertically – the top support hangs from the smoke box handrail, not from the lamp bracket as might be expected. The mounting brackets for the side arrows can also be seen on the smoke deflectors. Two changes have taken place since May 1952 – firstly much burnishing of fittings including handrails, lamp irons, smoke box door hinges, buffer heads, coupling shackles, piston head covers, pipe work etc. are all shined to perfection so Stewarts Lane's cleaning staff have been busy restoring the Festival of Britain finish. Secondly, the lower lamp irons have been extended and the head code discs will now sit approximately a foot above the buffer beam compared to previously. One wonders why? In this instance the tail lamp occupies the nearest bracket, ready for the short tender-first run down to Dover Marine station. Just visible to the left is LMS Fairburn 2-6-4 tank no. 42074.   *A. E. West R2010*

Opposite top - *Alongside the coaling plant again, in the same position as the lower view on p31 taken a year earlier but with Bulleid pacific No. 34099 "Lynmouth" in place of 30796. The mogul (or maybe a different one) is behind, carrying exactly the same head code, so possibly both locomotives are on the same diagrams. Railwaymen tended to be creatures of habit and followed the same routine wherever possible. Two sayings come to mind – "if it ain't broke, don't fix it" and (to paraphrase a little) "same service, different day!!"* A E. West R2009

Opposite bottom - *A rear view of No. 70004 on the same May 1953 occasion with the crew taking the opportunity to trim the coal during a brief sunny interlude. Four of the six lamp irons have been extended here as well, so maybe there had been an issue with lost discs? The two new SR ones are of a different pattern. Note much burnishing again and whitewashed vacuum and steam heating hoses! Just visible to the left is another Britannia tender but this is not the other SR allocated engine (no. 70014 "Iron Duke") but one of the seven on loan during the Merchant Navy crank axle crisis – it does not have the additional SR lamp irons but is still commendably clean nonetheless. Likely candidates are either 70030 "William Wordsworth" or 70034 "Thomas Hardy", temporarily allocated to Dover and Stewarts Lane respectively.* A. E. West R2011

Above - *No 70004 departing for Victoria at the head of a rake of twelve Pullmans, carrying VIP guests and others attending the Coronation of Queen Elizabeth II. The photographer recorded the time as 2.05pm and in pouring rain. Well, some things never change! On this day, presumably No. 70014 was in charge of the Golden Arrow. Perhaps appropriately, Shakespeare Cliff tunnel is behind the photographer.* A.E. West R2034

Top - The weather had improved (just) ten minutes later when Battle of Britain No. 34077 "603 Squadron" departed with a baggage train for the Royal visitors, consisting of a SECR "Continental" brake first in crimson lake and cream, a Pullman car and about five specially cleaned bogie utility vans. Despite the time of 2.15pm on a May day, the Bulleid's headlamps are illuminated.

A. E. West R2035

Middle - A few minutes later at 2.20pm we see a more usual train formation. N15 class No. 30770 "Sir Prianius" passes with a Charing Cross via Tonbridge service consisting of a Bulleid "cross-country" BRCW 3-set, four Maunsells and another Bulleid set on the rear.

A. E. West R2036

Bottom - A typical Kent local of the period. D1 class 4-4-0 No. 31246 leaves Dover for Ashford hauling a 60ft "Birdcage" trio-C set from the number series 567-72/74-629. This was actually the preceding service to no. 70004, at 1.35pm and no doubt would have been overtaken by the "Brit" at Ashford.

A. E. West R2033

The two 'Britannias' were transferred away to the London Midland Region in June 1958 and probably never saw the same level of attention again. Bulleid pacifics returned to the "Arrow" duty (often original Merchant Navies Nos. 35001/28 or rebuild 35015). More ordinary replacements for nos. 70004/14 at Stewarts Lane came in the form of 'class 5s' Nos. 73041/42. Nothing like as glamorous and these were never given anything like the same special treatment. Indeed, No. 73042 was soon to disgrace itself in the Eastbourne collision of 25th August 1958, while working the overnight sleeper train from Glasgow.

BASINGSTOKE - *Revisited*

Roger Simmonds

Previous text and illustrative instalments on Basingstoke by Roger Simmonds appeared in Nos. 3, 5 and 9 of 'The Southern Way'.

Roger has now unearthed more photographs from his collection which we are delighted to include.

Above - Widening east of Basingstoke recorded on 12 January 1902. This is bridge, No. 113 at Elvetham between Fleet and Winchfield, close to milepost 38. Final completion of the widening to provide four tracks between Woking Junction and Worting Junction was in December 1904.

Right - Winklebury signal box was located on the north side of the four lines between Basingstoke West and Worting Junction. Brought into use on 30 May 1897, its purpose was as a simple break-section box. It was replaced by IBS signals on all four lines from 20 March 1932. Within was a Stevens frame although the number of levers is not reported.

We knew this one existed - but could not access it! Arguably one of the best views of the west end at Basingstoke ever located, showing the down local and through platforms plus the Alton bay. What makes this one so special of course is the presence of the Alton train in the bay and in particular its make up - four / six wheel vehicles. (The engine is an 'O2' No 226.) The original is a postcard annotated as 'Terry Hunt, Photographer, Basingstoke' and is postmarked, 'London, 2 AM MR 2.05'. It was sent from an unsigned individual to a Miss E Fuller in Swaffham, and although partly illegible includes the words, "What do you think of our station, it is nearly as large as ….…" - unfortunately there is no word to end the sentence!

ngstoke, S.W. Ry.

BASINGSTOKE   8 JULY 1921

Above - *Basingstoke staff, July 1921, probably taken on the occasion of Station Master Albert Kneller being transferred to Southampton Docks. A farewell dinner was held at the Station Hotel - possibly the building in the background - although Roger comments this could equally be the SM's house. The Station Hotel was located in full view of the station offices and for this reason was not used by the staff under normal circumstances. Instead they would frequent the Great Western Hotel on the opposite side of the station…. .*

Left - *The effect of freak weather conditions on a telegraph pole in the down yard at Basingstoke. No date is given, although it is believed to have been sometime in the mid to late 1920s.*

Opposite top - *Main line duty for an Adams X6 No. 663 on 17 August 1929. The engine is seen entering Basingstoke at the head of a Bournemouth - Newcastle service comprising GCR excursion (?) stock, but what IS that third coach?*

H C Casserley

Opposite bottom - *On the same day, U class No. 613 is recorded in the down local platform on a west of England working, the engine having been in service for just 14 months. Milk churns are being loaded / unloaded by the first van: somewhat hard to comprehend today from what is a totally urban environment but this was some decades before the words 'London overspill', and which was responsible for so much development locally from the 1960s onwards. Just visible in the Alton bay is a solitary vehicle, whilst GW stock in the background indicate the presence of the opposition.*

H C Casserley

Opposite top - *D15 No 466 in the same platform as the 'U' class seen on the previous page but this time with what the headcode indicates is a Southampton Docks/ Terminus service. Completed at Eastleigh in July 1912, the engine received an Eastleigh superheater in March 1916 replaced by a Maunsell type in February 1926. Duty 282 was an Eastleigh Monday - Saturday turn involving the locomotive with following workings: fish vans to Portsmouth: Portsmouth - Romsey (reverse) - Eastleigh passenger: 11.58 am Eastleigh - Woking: (presumably now light engine to Waterloo), followed by the 3.54 pm Waterloo - Basingstoke passenger and finally the 6.50 pm Basingstoke - Southampton Terminus. The engine would likely have returned light to Eastleigh from Southampton. No timings or starting point are given for the fish vans or other workings. Of necessity, several sets of footplate men would have been involved.*

Opposite bottom - *Approaching Basingstoke from the east is S15 No. 30499 with a west of England freight. When cleared, the ground signal seen permitted movement across what was a considerable 'ladder crossing', the first portion of which is under the leading vehicles of the train. This crossed all four running lines plus the up siding terminating in Barton Mill (carriage) sidings, located the other side of the overbridge in the background.*

Above - *No 35022 'Holland-America Line' leaving Basingstoke with the 1.30 pm Waterloo to Bournemouth on 2 April 1955. In the background, No. 30860 'Lord Hawke' waits in the former Alton bay (not this time to head a train to Alton - the Alton branch had closed decades earlier), but instead for the coaches forming the 1.24 Waterloo - Salisbury, which it will take forward from this point. In the background is the massive water tower for the station. Notice the lack of signal wires: all low-pressure pneumatic control. Years later in 1966 the mechanical signalling was replaced by 'first generation' MAS - upper quadrant arms having already superseded the LSWR type seen. The former Alton bay was still in use for a while and therefore had a MAS signal controlling the exit on to the main line. Some time after the track and platform were considered redundant hence the rails were removed - but the MAS signal remained, starkly glowing red (the only indication it was possible to display) over a bed of ballast for well over a year following.*

Philip J Kelley

- and speaking of the 'Basingstoke & Alton' line (which was referred to in passing in the previous pages, these three still images from 'Oh Mr. Porter' recently surfaced. The story needs little introduction, so readers should not mind too much if at first we see Will Hay alongside an LNER 'A4', as indeed appeared at the start of the film.

Below is a view similar to, but certainly not the same, as appeared in the 'Basingstoke & Alton Light Railway' book. Will Hay is about to have his sleep interrupted in what was a mock-up of a railway carriage although the cow was the genuine article from a farm near to filming at Cliddesden.

Finally on the right Will Hay is seen in classic pose directing shunting. The late Harry Holcroft in his career biography 'Locomotive Adventure' refers to how the SR were approached and set up the railway sequences for the filming, many of the incidents totally impossible to replicate under 21st century safety legislation.

Which also leads us neatly on to…..

BASINGSTOKE (JUST)

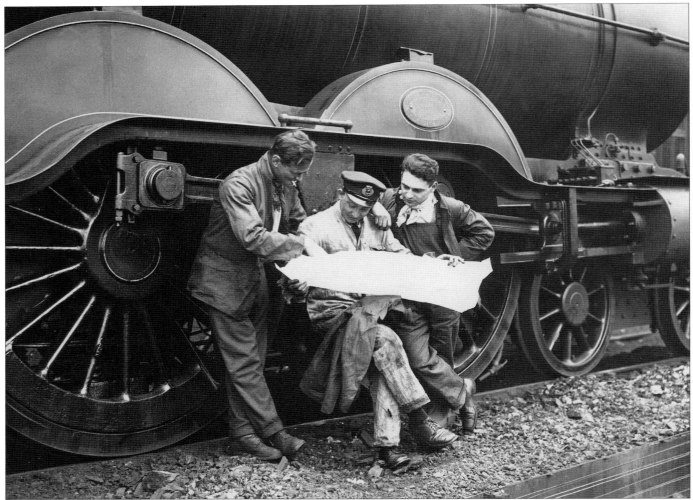

Above - This view we have had 'in stock' for a long time - and yes I know it is a Great Northern 'Atlantic' rather than as had been hoped, the LBSCR version. We include it as a press photograph taken at the time of the General Strike in 1926, when volunteer footplate crews, amongst others, were for two weeks able to 'play trains' to their hearts content. (Yes, in reality I know it was a bit better regulated than that.) Whatever, the newspaper image shows three such volunteers 'complete with a map'! I don't think we should take that one too literally.

Left - From the archives of the late John Hatherall comes this delightful staff snapshot. I love these type of views for they often show scenes of everyday life others fail to capture. All we know is it is definitely somewhere on the S & D, but the circumstances or occasion are not reported.

THE LIGHTER SIDE

In summer 2012 we published a book of light hearted (but all with a grain of truth) ditties on railways generally. *'GWR SIGNAL BOX CATS - Liveries and Allocations'.* Not intended to be a literal book related to the title alone, more on moggies and other similar off-beat tales (or should be 'tails'?) has since come to light. So without further ado...

How not to let pomposity overrule better judgment - by Ron Mason.

The appointment of young graduates into senior railway positions during the Doctor Beeching era caused resentment amongst staff in many sectors of the industry, not least "The Southern" where sometimes certain incidents created ridicule.

One such event occurred when a new young Divisional Manager arrived. It was not long before his high-handed approach allied to a general air of importance (which matched neither his knowledge nor experience) became known throughout.

Working in London but living in Basingstoke meant a daily commute, using the time to extol his personal and professional virtues to his city colleagues with whom he travelled - first class of course. This was also still the steam era, usually 'West Country Pacific' hauled

One morning they had not been progressing for long when the journey was interrupted by a sudden stop between Winchfield and Hook, caused, it was soon established, by the failure of a component within the engine valve gear.

The driver walked back to notify the guard and summon assistance, passing and acknowledging through the coach window two of his fellow footplate colleagues in the front compartment who were traveling back as passengers to Waterloo.

On reaching the guard at the rear of the train the driver explained the problem. It was also then that the guard remembered who was on board and felt he should of course notify his Divisional Manager as to exactly what had happened.

By this stage and egged on no doubt by his city friends intent on discovering the cause of the delay, our Managerial Buffoon went back of his own volition to find the guard.

The guard in the meanwhile had explained who the 'VIP' was who was traveling and so between them the two 'more established' railwaymen decided a bit of mileage could be obtained from this – at the expense of our friend of course. Consequently the driver explained in graphic detail the cause, position and consequence of the failure. Our friend

listened in silence seemingly taking it all in. At the end he pronounced, "No problem" said the Manager, no doubt thinking it would be his chance to shine said, "I will go through the train to identify my position and (now that he knew the exact problem) explain to passengers what had

This time we have a culprit, Jack Watton, Porter at Midford. I would not deem to pass comment upon what Jack may be pointing at in this undated view. I can only apologise that the size of the print makes enlargement impractical. (No we will not be supplying a free set of magnifiers with this issue - ED.)
John Hatherall

happened."

All went well to start, many passengers seemed mostly impressed by receiving information (and no doubt apologies) from such a high ranking official. Our friend no doubt thought (and hoped) such action might well prevent a host of complaints arriving on his desk subsequently.

Upon reaching the first compartment at the front of the train he noticed the train crew. "Ah!", he thought, "These men are traveling as passengers I might as well continue", especially as he had received no query so far. He was thus proud to share his new-found knowledge. "Well chaps" - and he started to recite the exact words quoted to him by the train driver, "There is a broken cotter pin behind the crank shaft on the left hand gear box.................". There was a moments silence after which one of the drivers who, having previously been tipped off by the engine crew, interrupted him and turned first to his colleague with a quizzical look and then back to the Manager, "Thanks guv for explaining, but tell me what exactly is the cotter pin behind the crank shaft on the left hand gear box….?"

The silence was measurable, after which came a somewhat rapid response, "Well er,. well er…I suggest you get the engine driver to explain whilst I go back through the train".

I feel sure this would have dented some misjudged enthusiasm.

THE LIGHTER SIDE

How to win friends and influence people (on the Southern) by Ron mason

This famous expression, originating from a successful American Entrepreneur, was certainly relevant for the railways during the 1950 and1960 periods and none less certainly on the Southern Region.

It was during this time that the system was being transformed, motive power wise there was the change from steam to ever more electrification (plus some diesel of course) but whilst this may have been welcomed by the travelling public, what was not were the many line closures occurring around the same time.

. For the railwaymen themselves it seemed as if experience no longer counted, groups of young academics appointed above the heads of traditional long-serving staff. Many of the former having little or no business experience and similarly little or no knowledge of railways in general.

Such was the case at an un-named south London office of the Southern Region where a new Divisional Manager had been appointed.

One floor of this building was also occupied by the large 'train operations' room, populated by a number of staff, mainly it must be said young men, but even so with both experience and also enthusiasm for railways. The team worked both happily and closely, organising train operating arrangements throughout their area.

Unfortunately it soon became clear that the arrival of this new senior manager was causing a rift. His attitude and sense of work ethic was not to their liking and many arguments followed. Matters eventually reached fever pitch at which point a group discussion between came up with the idea to try and retaliate against said individual in the hope that he might be moved.

How they achieved this has passed into folklore, no violence or intimidation, just experience and guile set against youth and arrogance.

Within the office one of their combined duties was to prepare the weekly 'Special Traffic Notices[1] which were then circulated to all operational staff from drivers to signalmen, station staff etc. These were known as the bible when it came to movements, their purpose being to highlight changes to the specified service published in the working timetable.

Christmas time was also approaching and elsewhere and at a much higher level, a decision that for the first time ever all services would be withdrawn on Christmas Day. The train staff were obviously pleased to be getting an extended holiday. But when the special traffic notice for the week was circulated and distributed instead of jubilation there was uproar from London as far as to the west Country, for upon turning the page after the final details for 24th December had appeared were details of a special train to run on Christmas morning, and which therefore requiring many operating staff to be in attendance.

The special was advised as running from North Pole Junction, and for the benefit of a Mr S Claus, a note added that reindeer were being loaded on board.

Many staff perhaps naively but with a sense of absolute *loyalty* started to prepare arrangements but at the same time expressing their complete disgust.

Not surprisingly news reached not just the new Divisional manager but also BR Headquarters by which time also the unions had become involved. The latter, seeing the apparent change from previously negotiated arrangements, considered there to be no alternative but to call an immediate strike.

Perhaps fortunately at this stage it began to be realised that the whole thing was a hoax but a hoax which had been carried out on a sacred document and one which had

108

Christmas Day, Friday, 25th December—continued

66—PARTIES (2nd Class).

NAME	Ref.	Adults	Children	FROM	TO	TRAINS Out	TRAINS Home	STATION TO RESERVE
Mr. S. Claus' Party	SB	1	12 Reindeer	North Pole Jn.	Dover Marine ...	00 01	—	North Pole Jn. (Parcels).

SB—Sleigh to be loaded in brake van. Mr. J. Frost to arrange assistance.

Opposite bottom - 'Dog Watch' (night shift) at Southampton.
Opposite top - If we can have 'Signal Box Cats' why can we not have 'Loco Shed Moggies' - but in what livery?
Above - They saying is, 'the camera cannot lie', although nowadays that may not be so strictly true with the various computer -imagining tools available. But then neither can the 'Special Traffic Notice' The original (undoctored) version for 25 December from Ron Mason.

49

casued much angst and anguish amongst staff.

Because it had happened 'on his watch' there was the rapid appointment of a new divisional manager. At which point also normal congenial staff arrangements resumed.

Needless to say (as had been anticipated by the planners), because of the joint responsibility in producing the weekly bulletin no one individual could be blamed.

One thing missing though was no mention in the STN as to whether mince pies would be collected at stopping points on route.

Table 215— HIGH DUDGEON, HAMTONBYSTED, THWAITE, and PELTING ST. GILES

Miles from High Dudgeon		Week Days a.m.	a.m.	a.m.	a.m.	p.m.	p.m.	p.m.		p.m.	p.m.	p.m.	p.m.	Suns. a.m.
	274 Stoke Poges .... dep	..	6 13	12z 3		..	3 14	..		..	3a40	..	2 15	10 30
	319 Haworth .... "	..	4 54	..		..	6 43	..		..	..	..	11m 3	10 30
	241 Tintagel .... "	..	..	4 13		C	2 30	..		..	2z18	..	12 13	10 30
	490 Stonehenge .... "	..	1 13	..			11z43	..		..	..	..	..	10 30
—	High Dudgeon .... dep	9 13	10 4	10 41	TC Tintagel to Barnsley, June 1 to 4	12 40	..	1 43	Wednesdays only May 25 to October 19	..	2 16	..	10 50	10 20
4½	Abbot's Lucre .... "	9 34	..	11 1		..	..	2 34		..		..	11 5	10 56
8	Prince's Lucre .... "	10 23	10 54	11 37		..	Via [illegible] Table 38 Commences June 6	1st class only Mons. & Fris.; 3rd class only Tues. & Thurs.; RC Mons. & Sats.; TC to Ley Fris. & Thurs.; 1st class Pullman Mons. & Sats.; 3rd Pullman Tues. & Thurs.; limited accommodation Thurs. & Fris. Buffet Car Tues. & Fris.		..	Terminates at Ford Mons. & Fris. Passengers change at 3.14	..	..	11 32
11¾	Cleobury Stonier .... "	11 1	..	11 56		..				λ		..	..	..
15½	Trapse-le-Street .... "	11 35	..	..		..				λ		..	..	..
20	King's Balsam G .... "	12 17	..	..		..				λ		..	12 17	The Sabbatarian RC Passengers take pot-luck
23¼	Hamtonbysted .... arr	12 41	12 50	12 46		12 50				..		..	12 43	
—	Devizes .... arr	Stop		2 15		3 1				..		..		
—	430 Stoke Poges .... arr	2a13	The Village Hampden TC Stoke Poges to Kyle of Lochalsh	12 47		..				..		g	SC Abbot's Lucre to K's Balsam U	
—	245 Tintagel .... "	..		..		..				..		..		
—	372 Haworth .... "	..		..		..				..		Uu		
—	Hamtonbysted .... dep	..		12 56		1252				..		..		
27	Worth .... "	..		..		..				..		Kk		
31¼	Ford .... "	3 45		..		..				3 14		..		
34	Ley .... "	4 13		..		The Suffix Belle TC RC & SC High Dudgeon to London (Paddington)				..	Terminates at Gate Tues. & Sats. Passengers change at 6.18	..		
37¼	Ings .... "	5 53		..			12 58			..		..		
41	Thorpe Platform .... "	Stop		1 29			1 23			Stop		..		
41½	Cote Halt .... "	..		1 34			1 53			..		..		
44	Cester .... "	..		..			..			4 16		g		..
48¼	Thwaite .... arr	..		2 10			TC Bletchley to Oldham (Clegg St.)			4 53		..	3a14	..
—	Warminster .... arr	..		The Backwoodsman RC Thorpe Platform to Cote Halt except Weds. Q						Passengers for beyond Stoke Poges change at Thwaite for Norwich (Thorpe)		g	..	6 30
—	453 Stoke Poges ...... arr	..										..	..	6 30
—	349 Stonehenge .... "	..										..	..	6 30
—	Thwaite .... dep	4 16										..	3a17	..
53	Hurst .... "	7/40										..		..
56¾	Holt .... "	4 51										..		..
60	Field .... "	..										..		Hh
64¼	Gate .... "	Uu										6 18		..
67¼	Borough .... "	UuKk									Not Weds. & Thurs.	..	The Night Watchman t	..
69	Mouth .... "	Pp	..			..						..		..
71	Beck .... "	..	..			..						Stop		..
73¼	Toft .... "	..	9p48			..						..		..
76	Gill .... "	..	UuKk			..						..		..
79	Well .... "	..	..	..		..	..	..				..	..	..
84¼	Wish .... "	..	..	..		..	..	..				..	..	..
88	Dale .... "	..	..	..		..	..	11 17				..	..	..
91¼	Pelting St. Giles ..... arr	!!	11z40	6p48J		1 43	!!	12 47			2d43z	..	5 19	6 30
—	141 London (Pad.) .... arr	..	..	!!		2 15	4a2T	..		..	..	..	!!	..
—	411 Stonehenge .... "	11q3	..	..		8q43	..	..		..	..	..	..	..
—	308 Stoke Poges .... "	..	..	..		11 51	..	..		..	..	..	..	..

NOTES

- a a.m.
- C Suspended
- d By slip carriage
- G Station for Friar's Balsam 1¼ miles
- g Ten minutes *earlier* on Fridays
- Hh Not on Sundays !
- λ Single-line working during derailments
- J Next Friday
- j The compilers are not sure of this
- Kk Does not take up
- m Previous morning
- Pp Stops for wheel-tapping if complaint made to guard at previous *stopping* station
- p p.m.
- Q Carries a fine Château d'Yquem, 1928
- q Passengers cross from Stonehenge (Cromlech) to Stonehenge (Piltdown) by means of an aerial ropeway
- RC Refreshment car
- SC Sleeping accommodation
- T Depends upon arrival time at Pelting St. Giles
- t Hard seats
- TC Through carriages
- U Sleeping-car passengers must be out and about by 3 a.m.
- u Passengers not allowed to bring own food
- Uu Does not set down
- z Night

Above *- Ron Mason also kindly submitted the above which he says was circulating around the Railway Enthusiasts Club 50 or so years ago. Proof if proof were needed about the sanity of our hobby.*

Left *- 'Egg-cellent'*

A PAIR OF OLD BOILERS

Steve Godden has been in touch recently with some amazing images from his time working as a plumber and gas fitter on the Southern Region - all part of the essential 'behind the scenes' activities of an organisation that on the surface at least was there solely to 'run trains'. Steve has promised us an article shortly but in the meanwhile two gems from his collection showing what were described as 'old heating boilers' at Brighton Works. The date is not given although we suspect sometime in the 1950s. The only indication is the 'SB29' shown on the

firebox which must stand for 'Stationary boiler No 29'. Clearly ex-locomotive, but any ideas which? The firing point complete with covering is interest, so who would have been deputized to attend to the engine - and equally where is the chimney?

Rudyard Kipling and the 'Brighton'

Alastair Wilson

In 1899, the author Rudyard Kipling was living in Rottingdean, and made use of the Brighton line for his trips to London, and elsewhere in Sussex. Like many other Sussex dwellers, he didn't go much on 'the Brighton': it was only three years earlier that E.L. Ahrons had written 'The Crawl to the South' as a counterpoint to the enthusiasm for the 1895 'Race to the North'. And later on Ahrons wrote scathingly of the Brighton of this period in the LBSCR section of 'Locomotive and Train Working in the Latter Part of the Nineteenth Century', which appeared in *The Railway Magazine* from 1915 to 1921 (the Brighton piece appeared in 1919).

In 1901, Kipling wrote a piece, which was published in *The Fortnightly Review* of February 1901, entitled 'Railway Reform in Great Britain'. This was a skit, written as though it was a translation from ancient Persian – rather in the manner that the tales of 'The Arabian Nights' were told, and it concerned the iniquities of the Brighton.

Ahrons had written, among much else, "But truth compels me to say that I do not think that the denizens of the London Bridge offices contributed very much to its popularity; they were a cheerful band of railway sinners, more especially those connected with the traffic department, and between them they could then produce more chaotic unpunctuality than could be found anywhere, except perhaps on the South Eastern. Luckily the geographical position of the Brighton line limited the length of the journeys. Had the company to deal with a longer main line, it is just conceivable that some of their nineteenth century trains might just be arriving at their destinations today. Moreover, the best trains were for first-class, or first and second-class passengers only, and the poor third class traveller generally had a benighted time."

This is a flavour of what Kipling wrote: "Then they went into the caravanserai appointed for the coming and the departure, and it was as though a battle had passed that way; for the caravanserai was full of smoke, black and white, and the ground was piled with the baggage of the faithful - pots, and bundles, and food, and medicaments, and the implements of exercise and diversion, all in little heaps, and by each heap stood distressful women and children not a few, imploring guidance. Hereupon the Caliph enquired: 'What have these done to merit extinction?' And Giaffar replied: 'They go a journey in the brazen engines,' and he recited the following verses:- 'The Mercy of Allah is upon all things created, whereby the ignorant emerge from vicissitude: If it seem good in the eyes of the Fashioner of Events, doubt not that these, even these, shall ultimately arrive at their destination.'

Then came a servant of the Afrit clad in bluish raiment, and cried: With thy permission!' and smote the legs of Giaffar from under him by means of a small wheeled cart which he wheeled in haste, and he recited the following verses:- 'O True Believers! The first is behind the third, and the third is before the second. Advance boldly and turn to the right! Continue and turn to the left, for that brazen engine which departs for Lawaz and Isbahan upon the hour of second prayer lacking one eighth of an hour. Come hither, O true Believers, and behold the brazen engine which departs for Raidill: but go elsewhere if thou wouldst behold the towers of Harundill! Ya Illah! Allah! Six is four and three is five; but the second and third are only little engines from Sha'ham.'"

This is a description of Brighton station, and when

We have recently been privileged to be granted access to the collection of glass plates from the collection of the late E E Wallis, comprising scenes and signalling mainly on the Southern but some also from elsewhere. Most of these are originals but there are also others collected by a man who besides being a perceptive photographer was keen to gather what early material was available even then. (Continued opposite)

you've got yourself attuned to the mock-Persian, you will realise that Lawas is Lewes; Isbahan is Eastbourne; Raidill is Redhill; Harundill is Arundel; and Sha'ham is Shoreham. The "brazen engines" are of course Stroudley's and Billinton's, still (most of them anyway) in Stroudley's lovely 'improved Engine Green'; while the 'servant of the Afrit, clad in bluish raiment' is a porter with his cry of 'By y'r leave', when he wanted to get by with his platform barrow ('small wheeled cart.').

Kipling's piece is too long to reproduce here, and besides, there is probably quite a lot of it which would not be readily understood by those born after 1950. However, all is not lost, anyone with access to the world-wide web, whether on their own account or with the help of a grandchild, can find a complete text, with interpretation, at www.kiplingsociety.co.uk (access is free to all). This will bring up the Kipling Society's home page: click on 'Reader's Guide', and then on 'Uncollected Stories': that will bring up a list of Kipling's writings which weren't collected into one or another of his books: in the left-hand column of writings which appear in red, will be found <u>Railway Reform in Great Britain</u>. Click on that, and there you are, with a reproduction of one of C. Hamilton Ellis's paintings of a Craven single on the Cuckoo Line. In the top right-hand corner of that page is a link to the Kipling text, another to the notes and interpretation of that text and another to Ahron's diatribe against the Brighton.

This author thinks it makes a fascinating bit of railway history.

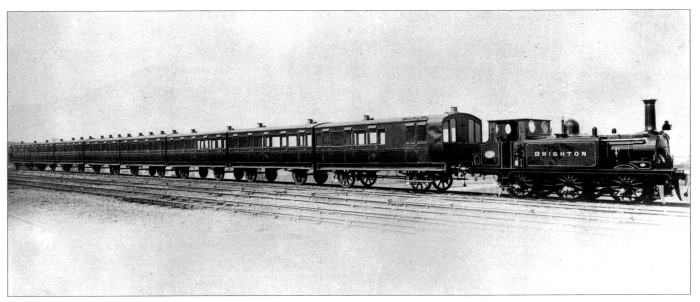

Opposite page - *The viaduct at Brighton, undated but believed to be sometime in the 1870s.*
Top - *Down Brighton train passing Balham intermediate.*
Above - *Engine No. 40, appropriately named 'Brighton' but shown with a set train for the south London line.*

The new locomotive ex works in workshop grey. Altogether an admirably proportioned design of distinctive and pleasing appearance.

MAUNSELL'S THREE CYLINDER 'N1' PROTOTYPE

Martin Breakspear

Nothing sounds worse than a steam engine with poorly set valve events. Valve systems used on railway steam engines involve compromises in terms of ideal valve events, and the differing systems involve a different set of compromises. Stephenson gear gives variable lead, Walschaerts gives constant lead. Straight link Allan, Joy, Baker's and others offer a similar diversity of problems and solutions to getting steam in and out of the cylinders. In all of these, problems with angularity of the links, cylinder layout and available space force compromises on the designer, and assessing these compromises demanded a major effort in the design offices of all locomotive builders. Good valve events are a very necessary result for efficiency and free running.

The extensive use by Sir Nigel Gresley on the LNER of his conjugated valve gear to drive the centre cylinder valve by a derived motion is well known. In good mechanical condition it worked well enough to claim the world steam speed record. The syncopated beat of a Gresley locomotive is recognisable anytime, even when the gear is fresh out of shops. When badly worn, however, it is a very different story. Wear in the bushes in the 2:1 arm and associated linkage led to overrunning of the centre valve, giving a disproportionate power delivery from the centre cylinder. In addition, the valve events became out of sequence from the piston position, thus leading to an awful out of sync sounding exhaust. In a way it was no surprise that Thompson and then Peppercorn discarded the conjugated arrangements for a set of valve gear for each cylinder.

However, the conjugated gear did offer a number of solutions to the everlasting problem of fitting all of the motion in to the very constricted space that the standard gauge locomotive offered between the frames. On a divided drive 3-cylinder locomotive, that is, one with the inside cylinder driving the leading axle and the two outside cylinders on the middle axle, there is no simple solution to deriving a valve drive from the outside valves to the centre valve. Gresley considered that a separate valve gear for the centre cylinder cost weight, and his conjugated valve gear was an elegant engineering solution to the problem. Gresley first patented his design in 1915, and used it subsequently on all of his major locomotives.

What is not so well known, is that an engineer on the Great Western Railway, Harold Holcroft, had first proposed a patent for a conjugated valve gear in 1909. Holcroft was one of Churchward's shining stars, and was responsible for, amongst many other good things, what became the definitive GWR standard style of locomotive, with the curved front and rear running plates. Holcroft was known to have assisted Gresley in developing his conjugated gear, which must have been to Holcroft's benefit as Churchward eschewed 3-cylinder layouts, preferring 2- and 4-cylinder locomotives, thus denying him the opportunity to try it out in full size on his home railway. Holcroft built a working model of a 4-4-0 locomotive utilising this gear and he showed it to Gresley. This model is now in the possession of the GWR Museum Trust at Didcot.

Once Churchward had developed his standard range of locomotive designs, his engineering team was increasingly used on non-locomotive and secondary locomotive work, and this was obviously not to Holcroft's liking. He left the GWR in 1914 and joined Maunsell's team on the SECR. This was an interesting move, as although he enjoyed much more freedom under Maunsell, the Maunsell team was a somewhat conservative one, preferring well-tested and proven ideas rather than new ones, and Holcroft was definitely a new ideas man. What is clear is that Gresley formed a favourable impression of Holcroft, and tried to persuade him to join the GNR team. There apparently ensued a big row between Maunsell and Gresley, resulting in Holcroft remaining with the SECR. Nevertheless, the subsequent route that the SECR, and then Southern, steam engine design took mirrors the modernistic Churchward approach of Belpaire fireboxes, taper boilers, and long travel valves. Holcroft's influence must have been there, and I suspect that his recruitment by Maunsell does suggest an open mind on his, Maunsell's, part anyway, to new ideas that had been proven elsewhere. It also seems that one outcome of this was that Holcroft got the opportunity to develop and build an example of his conjugated valve gear. The resulting locomotive was 2-6-0 No. 822, class N1. Subsequently, the K1 class 2-6-4T No. 890 in was built in 1925, and had very similar valve gear details to the N1.

Ashford Works turned out No. 822 in late 1922, and it was reported in the Railway Engineering press in the New Year after the formation of the Southern Railway. Maunsell was given the job of Chief Mechanical Engineer of the Southern, a role he fulfilled until retirement on grounds of ill health in 1937. Holcroft remained with Maunsell and carried on under Bulleid, a boss, one would have thought, Holcroft would have worked well with as an ideas man.

No. 822 was similar in appearance to the previous 2

-cylinder N class engines, with which it shared the smokebox, (slightly altered to take a bigger chimney) boiler, frame, wheels, coupling and connecting rods, brakes and cab designs, (the cab front was slightly different). The major difference was that it was a three cylinder locomotive, rather than two, with the boiler pitched higher than on the N to clear the centre cylinder. All three cylinders drove the centre coupled axle. Associated with the inside cylinder was a novel application of Holcroft's conjugated drive. The design had a significant difference to Gresley's layout, as explained later. The importance of the third cylinder was that it allowed smaller outside cylinders for the same tractive effort, thus a reduced loading gauge gave wider route availability

The engine part of the locomotive was as follows. Two outside cylinders, 16 inches diameter by 28 inches stroke mounted horizontally drove the centre axle. 8-inch piston valves arranged for long travel gave good steam entry and exhaust. The valves were actuated directly by Walschaerts valve gear, with the motion carried forward from the rear of the cylinders to a conjugated arrangement across the front of the engine. The third cylinder of similar dimensions and valve design, was fitted between the frames at an inclination of 1 in 8 to allow the connecting rod and crosshead to clear the leading axle to drive on the centre axle. The centre cylinder valve was driven indirectly by the two outside valve gears combined in the 2:1 cross arm with a secondary 1:1 arm to form a conjugated motion from which a drive to the centre valve spindle was taken. The net effect, combined with the angular setting of the crank axle to the outside crank pins, was to give a synchronised motion to the valve to admit and exhaust steam from the centre cylinder. To accommodate the inclined inside cylinder, the inside crank setting was 113 deg to the right hand crank pin, and 127 to the left hand crank pin. All three connecting rods were the same length. This feature, along with the nominal 120 deg. crank setting gives perfect balancing of the engine for reciprocating and most of the revolving masses. Only the external coupling rods demand balancing, and in fact Bulleid eschewed balancing on his pacifics as being unnecessary. In the case of the Nl, of course this benefit was not wholly obtained as the cranks are not exactly at 120 deg. Pretty close enough however to give a smooth ride.

The leading dimensions of the locomotive were as follows, set alongside the N class dimensions:

	Three-Cylinder N1	Two-Cylinder N
Cylinders		
Diameter	16 inches	19 inches
Piston Stroke	28 inches	28 inches
Piston valves		
Inside Admission	3 valves, 8 inch diameter	2 valves, 10 inch diameter
Maximum Travel	5 inches	6⅞ inches
Wheels		
Front Bogie (bissel truck)	3 feet 1 inch diameter	3 feet 1 inch diameter
Coupled	5 feet 6 inches diameter	5 feet 6 inches diameter
Heating Surfaces		
Firebox	135 sq.ft.	135 sq.ft.
Tubes	1390.6 sq.ft.	1390.6 sq.ft.
Total	1525.6 sq.ft	1525.6 sq.ft
Superheater (21 elements)		
Grate Area	25 sq.ft.	25 sq.ft.
Working Pressure	190 psi.	200 psi.
Tractive Effort at 80% boiler pressure	11 tons	10.9 tons
Total Weight		
Engine in working order	62 tons 15 cwt	59 tons 8 cwt
On coupled wheels	53 tons	50 tons 18 cwt
Tender		
Wheel Diameter	4 feet	4 feet
Coal capacity	5 tons	5 tons
Water capacity	3,500 gallons	3,500 gallons

Seen from the opposite side, two views of No. 822 and in 'as built' condition. It will be noted the engine is right-hand drive.

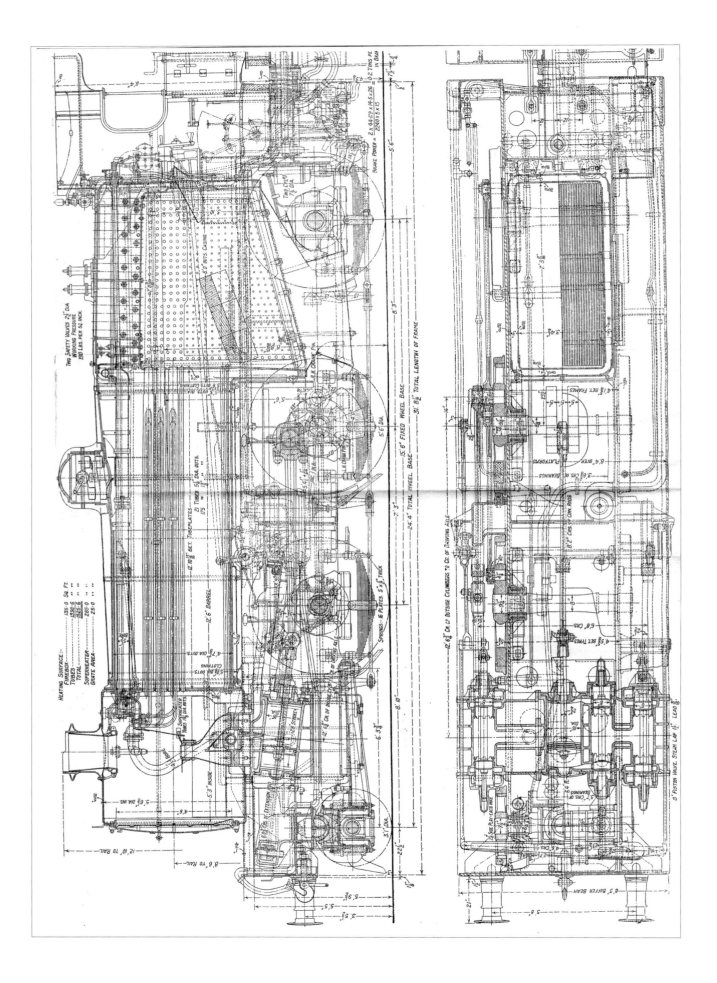

Opposite page - The drawing is the front half of the GA for the whole engine: as usual for the period it is an exquisite piece of draftsmanship. The inclination of the centre cylinder can be seen, and the connecting link (extension rod) from the outside cylinder valve spindle to the conjugating arm passes across the outside of the outside cylinder at an inclined angle. An important difference between Holcroft's design and Gesley's, was that because the drive from the outside cylinders was on the rear (cold) side of the valves, any expansion of the outside valve spindles as the engines warmed up did not cause an alteration of the middle valve settings. There was also the bonus that if there was any need to withdraw the valves, it was not necessary to dismantle the conjugating motion for the outside cylinders, thus reducing shed costs.

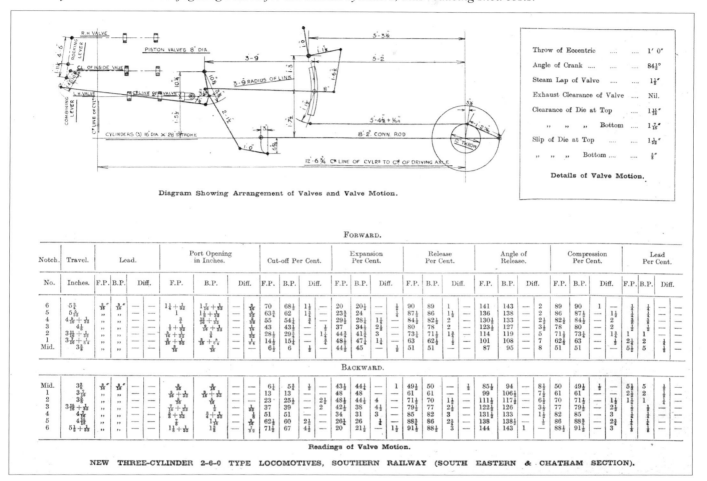

Diagram Showing Arrangement of Valves and Valve Motion.

Details of Valve Motion.

Readings of Valve Motion.

NEW THREE-CYLINDER 2-6-0 TYPE LOCOMOTIVES, SOUTHERN RAILWAY (SOUTH EASTERN & CHATHAM SECTION).

The original reduction of working pressure appears to be solely to give the same tractive effort across both classes. The additional weight on the coupled wheels of the Nl class, plus the more even torque delivery of the three-cylinder arrangement compensates for the additional effort of the third cylinder, and so perhaps it was an odd decision. On rebuilding, and for the new builds, the pressure was restored to 200psi ,thus giving the extra benefit of increased haulage power. The figures clearly show that the only difference in the engines apart from the extra cylinder, was the cylinder and valve dimensions, and so the main benefit of the design from an operational point of view would have been the extra route availability.

The working of the inside valve gear needs some thought to understand what is happening. Looking at the simple diagram below, we see the 2:1 arm (rocking lever) driven by the Right Hand outside gear, and the 1:1 arm (combining lever)driven by the Left Hand gear. Remembering that on this three cylinder locomotive, the cranks are arranged when looking towards the front of the locomotive from the cab, that the order of lead is Right hand crank, Left hand crank, Middle crank, and so on going forward.

The valve gear follows this order of course. Visualise now the 2:1 lever driven by the Right Hand gear. When the Right Hand gear is at full travel, it is effectively stopped momentarily. The motion of the Left hand gear now pivots the 1:1 arm about its pivot A. When the left hand gear is at full travel, ie stopped momentarily, the Right Hand gear is moving the 2:1 arm about the fixed pivot B, and thus moving the pivot point A of the 1:1 arm. Consider now what is happening to the pivot C in the 1:1 arm. This moves in synchronisation with the Left Hand gear.

More difficult to visualise now is what the centre arm motion is when both outside gears are moving. Essentially, it is a combination of the two movements, but remember that at some points in the cycles both gears are moving forwards (or backwards) together and at other points in the cycle they will be moving in opposite directions. There will be two points where the pivot point connected to the centre valve spindle will be momentarily stopped, that is, when the valve spindle is at the end of its travel and about to return. The result is a conjugated or combined motion of the

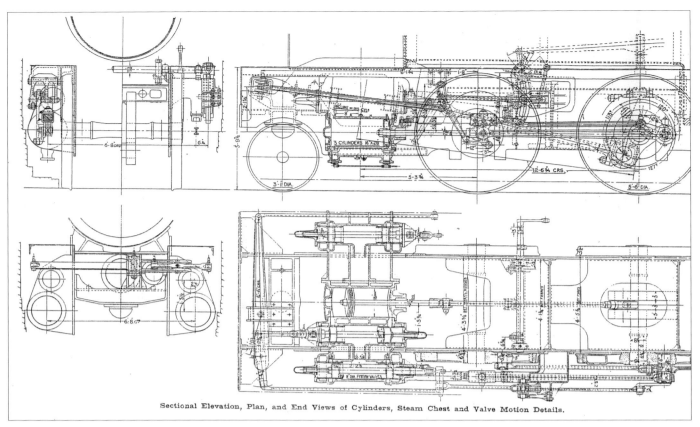

Sectional Elevation, Plan, and End Views of Cylinders, Steam Chest and Valve Motion Details.

The diagram makes the valve gear easier to see without the added GA detail. The drawing shows the closest proximity of the inside connecting rod to the leading axle. What is clear is the amount of space between the frames with this arrangement compared with having all of a third set of valve gear to contend with. The diagram shows the conjugated layout diagrammatically for ease of understanding, and the drawing shows the actual layout as built. A further diagram illustrates the valve gear layout diagrammatically. The table of dry looking numbers illustrates the point that all valve gear layouts are compromises, differences in performance between forward and back gear being seen. However, in a locomotive designed for express passenger work, the forward gear would have been optimised to give best results. If they can be found, the valve events and the expansion diagrams for the Ns would make for interesting comparison. Perhaps somebody out there has them for a future article

Brand new No. 878, one of the batch of five built in 1930 but without the conjugated valve drive. (No. 822 was similarly modified in the form seen at its next overhaul. This and other engines of the type had '1000' added to their numbers in 1931. Chimneys varied, almost it seemed from new, both 'U1' and 'Ashford' types noted.

MAUNSELL'S THREE CYLINDER 'N1' PROTOTYPE

No 31877 at Tonbridge in almost final BR guise. From photographs it does not appear any were ever AWS fitted whilst smokebox snifting valves were removed during Mr Bulleids's tenure. Most of their work was centred upon the South Eastern and later Brighton lines, operating both passenger and freight turns. Withdrawal came under the massive cull of late 1962 although a number were laid up for some months after this time. There would be no reprieve. J Davenport

centre valve spindle in relation to the two outside gears, that is, a motion that is sequenced by the relative motions of the outside gears: not easy to visualise. But properly set up, the valve motion of the inside cylinder replicates the valve motion of the two outside valves to give ideally identical steam admission and release from the centre cylinder.

The simplified GA shows more clearly what the design was, but also illustrates how it was necessary sometimes to shoehorn things in to achieve a working solution to the conflicting restraints of space, layout and accessibility. The design does leave a lot of space inside the frames compared with a third set of valve gear, and even on a three-cylinder locomotive oiling up inside can be quite demanding on one's suppleness!.

It can be seen that good relative motions depends very much on the tightness of the various joints, and this was the major downfall of the conjugated motions. Once wear has set into the pins and bushes, the slack starts to distort the relative movements of the arms, and is accentuated by arm ratios.   The result is that as the locomotive approaches shopping, the valve events drift significantly away from the ideal and the locomotive becomes inefficient.

The performance of the locomotive is interesting. It appears that there was not a lot of difference in the performances of the N and the Nl in haulage power, the smaller cylinders on the Nl balanced by the extra cylinder input. What is strange however, is that in comparative trials on long goods train on the SE routes, more water was used but less coal by the Nl. This seems odd, in that more water needs more heat to boil it, hence more coal. It suggests that in fact the N class had deficiencies not fully realised. As an engineer it would have been a challenge to get to the bottom of these discrepancies, but clearly at the time the performances were satisfactory to the Southern management.

The most significant matter was the maintenance

costs of the locomotive. Over all, it appears that the Nl cost less than the Ns. The use of three cylinders gave a balanced engine, with little hammer blow on the rail and a smooth ride for the crew, even at speed. The Nl was capable of speeds in the high 70s. The conjugated gear unfortunately presented all of the maintenance problems experienced with conjugated design. Difficulties with lubrication led to excessive wear, compounded operationally by it being a one-off with no volume of spare parts being available. Once wear had set in, valve events were affected leading to unbalanced power delivery between the inside and outside cylinders because of uneven steam distribution. In addition, it was suspected that the conjugated arms whipped at high speed, making the valve events even worse. The spares situation might have altered had the Sevenoaks disaster not have happened. A Kl 2-6-4 tank with the conjugated valve gear was built and also performed well. Further Kls were to have been built, but the orders were cancelled due to the lack of confidence in the 2-6-4 tank locomotive ability to deal with Southern track quality.

The Nl, No. 822 remained a singleton until 1930, but its overall performance justified a further build of 5 locomotives being undertaken. The issues with the conjugated valve drive were resolved by discarding it and fitting a separate Walschaerts gear in between the frames for the inside cylinder in the new builds, other design features remaining the same. Boiler pressure was raised to 200 psi, and No. 822 was modified to the same layout at its next major overhaul.

The class performed well until the demise of steam in the 60s, when all 6 went together in 1962. Sadly, none are preserved. To my eye the Maunsell 2-6-0's were a well balanced looking design, with or without smoke deflectors, and we do at least have some of his other 2-6-0 classes persevered for us to enjoy.

"A PAIR OF BRACES"

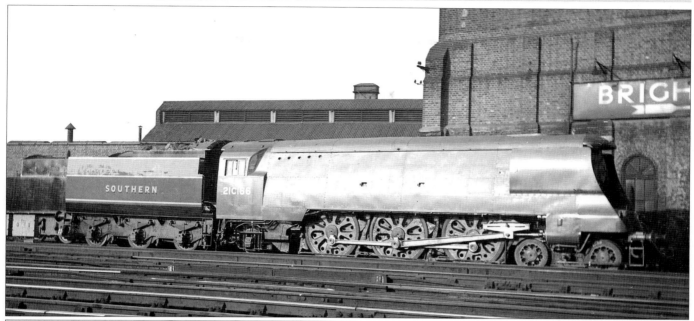

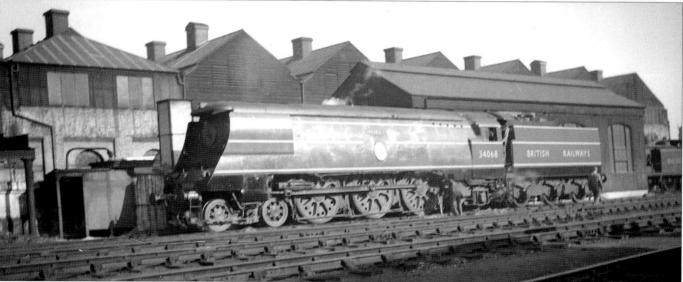

*Bulleids at Brighton in 1947/48. **Opposite top** is 21C165 'Hurricane' new from the nearby works on 8 July 1947 and recorded on 9 September 1947. The fact it has the works shunter positioned behind, does this indicate a possible return for attention? **This page, top** - 21C166, later 'Spitfire', unpainted on 9 August 1947, three weeks before it was reported as 'new to traffic': 5 September 1947. A completed and laden tender is coupled, so possibly this was reference a test run. **Opposite bottom** we see No. 21C167 'Tangmere' on 10 September 1947, exactly one week after official completion. Unfortunately the identity of the engines either side was not reported. Finally **this page bottom** is the renumbered 34068 'Kenley'. 'The Book of the West Country and Battle of Britain Pacifics' has this engine as having been returned to works for unspecified defects three times (twice to Brighton and once to Ashford) between 9 October 1947 and 30 September 1948. The first of these when the engine was just two days old and had amassed only 24 miles. By the time this view was taken on 30 September 1948, the engine was in steam after the third works visit, the opportunity having also taken to change the number to BR style. At this stage the recorded mileage had been 35,555 in one year. All four engines were allocated new to Ramsgate.*

(If you are wondering why 'A Pair of Braces', a 'brace' is two and two braces must therefore equal a pair……..)

Ancient and modern at Eastleigh, 1 February 1964. A grimy No. 73170 against the long afternoon shadows outside the back of Eastleigh shed. In the background by the side of the diesel depot reposes D6540.

Tony Molyneaux

PART 1 appeared in Issue No. 20

THE LAST STEAM-AGE FIREMAN PART 2

Roger Andrews

In 1962 Roger Andews started at Eastleigh Shed as a cleaner.
His was to be a brief sojourn on the railway, progressing to fireman
before leaving for differing pastures.
As such he is well qualified to recall his memories as
one of the last steam age firemen.

A couple of weeks after that incident, I took my place in the ashpan gang, as it was called, and officially became a fireman. I had enjoyed the last three months despite being derailed, but I was a bit apprehensive because I knew that once in the ashpan gang I would be likely to be confined to the shed for at least the next year. As it turned out I wasn't and I did get out and about quite a bit. The way this came about was simply that I became friendly with a more senior fireman who wanted to change turns now and again. I also got collared quite often, mostly at night, when the running foreman had run out of spare firemen. If my memory serves me right, the ashpan gang consisted of eleven or twelve sets of men, most of the drivers elderly and who had come off the main line for health reasons, the few younger ones probably colour-blind cases.

My own driver was one Jimmy Thomas, a real character who had come down from Nine Elms before the war. He was only about five feet tall and thin as a bean pole. Added to this was a long pointed nose whilst a mop of white hair always stuck out from under his 'grease top' railway cap which used to rest on his ears making him look much older than his 63 years. If you had given him a white cloak and a scythe he could easily have been 'old father time'. His health problem was some condition with his legs, which meant he used to shuffle along at about half a mile an hour; he also rode a big old-fashioned bike which went at the same speed. When walking around the shed together I was often tempted to pick him up and stick him under my arm. I was well over six feet tall and being young always went everywhere at a run.

When we were working on the pits on the 2 - 10 shift he quite often used to disappear for an hour. One day I asked one of the other drivers "Where does old Jimmy always get to?" "Oh, he goes up the betting shop by the station", he replied. I knew he was always very keen on the horses and that explained his hour-long absences as well as the time taken to get there and back.

In quieter moments Jimmy would tell me wonderful stories about the past. He also taught me the card game known as 'bennies', which was played by every footplate man wherever you found him. In fact one day in the 1970s coming back from London on the train I came across a group of footplate men travelling as passengers, and, yes, you've guessed it, they were playing bennies. I almost asked if I could join in but I don't think my wife would have approved. Jimmy was a real gent and I remember him with great affection.

There were two sets of men on the disposal pit and another set who berthed the engines in the shed. This was done in three shifts: early, late and nights. Thus this took care of nine sets of men, plus another set on 'shed-engine' which was only an afternoon turn, plus one preparation and disposal turn.

The men on the pits moved the engines along the pits all the time, but it was not that straight-forward because they were all having their fires cleaned. Most firemen were reluctant to move an engine in the middle of cleaning the fire or smokebox, so occasionally we had an empty disposal pit and six or so engines queued up between the turntable and the top of the disposal pit, but we would get them all down eventually.

As you moved them down you took water at one of the two water columns and raked out the engines' ashpans. There were still quite a few 'N' and 'U' class, or 'Woolies' as we called them, plus S15 type engines, about at this time. And it also seemed to make no difference which way the wind was blowing or which end of the ashpan you started from, you always got covered in ash which went down your neck, in your eyes and nose - in fact it got everywhere. Finally we moved the engine down to the steam crane to be coaled. The coaling stage was never used in my time at Eastleigh; in fact I don't think it had been used for years. I can never remember the drivers getting involved much in this entire engine moving, we firemen were just left to get on with it. The coaling gang numbered four, the driver of the steam crane, who seemed to be in charge, and the three others who did all the shovelling. The coal was shovelled

Rebuilt and original Bulleids at the back of the steam shed. Nos. 34042 'Dorchester', and 34091 'Weymouth'. The building on the left behind the locos is the sand drier.   *Mark Abbott*

from the wagon door into two steel tubs which must have held four or five hundredweight of coal.

When a new wagon of coal was started, the tubs would be parked near the wagon, the wagon door was then opened and dropped down; whatever coal fell out was soon shovelled up and went in the nearby tubs. Because the coal had been compacted on its journey, very little actually fell out when the door was released and there was usually a solid wall of coal. The tubs were then parked in front of the open door and shovelling commenced. The one thing guaranteed to upset the coalmen however, was to have a couple of wagon loads of ovoids. These were egg-shaped stove nuts of compressed coal about the size of a fist: they were made from crushed coal bound with cement and came from somewhere in Wales. The problem with the ovoids was that because of their uniform shape they did not compact so when the wagon door was dropped about a quarter of the contents would pour out onto the ground, which of course then all had to be shovelled up before the tubs could be positioned in front of the wagon for loading. I don't know if the ovoids were an economy measure but we always had a steady supply of them mixed in with the regular coal.

When full, the tubs were hoisted up by the crane and positioned over the tender. Using a long steel rod with a hook on the end, the crane driver pulled a catch on the tub, the bottom opened, and the contents deposited itself, complete with a cloud of dust, into the tender. When the tub was dropped back on the ground the bottom latched itself. The coalmen did have a sort of shelter to work under but it

was very high because it had to clear the jib of the crane and only covered half the wagon they were working from, it gave very little protection from the elements. To see a bunch of miserable coal men was to see them on a wet and stormy night, soaking wet and covered in coal dust, I would not have wanted to do their job for anything, they really did earn their money.

If the pair who were berthing the engines in the shed were on the ball, they would be waiting by the steam crane ready to move the engine away as soon as it had been coaled. Upon signing on, the driver of this pair would have picked up a shed plan, each engine allocated a slot in the shed in the right order for going off shed again. Engines that needed turning were marked 'Head Up' or 'Head Down', and would then have to go around the triangle to turn. This shed plan was constantly updated by the running foreman as more engines came on shed. It was always a case of the driver taking one engine and the fireman the next one.

Going past the steam crane, the track continued down a long straight about three hundred yards as far as the pointsman's hut which was at the end of the loco yard. We never went past this hut without stopping and speaking to the pointsman, and there was always a man on duty here at all times, day and night. As you stopped you shouted the number of the road you wanted. He would hold you there if there was already a movement in the yard, then let you go when it was safe for you to proceed. He would then go and set the road into the shed.

Disposal duty on '700' No. 30689 at Eastleigh.   *Mark Abbott*

From the pointsman's hut you could go on for another hundred yards as far as a 'dummy' which protected the entrance to the triangle and also the back of the diesel depot. If the signal cleared you had gone through a set of sprung points, from here you went back to the shed. If it was needed to use the triangle to turn, it was necessary to wait at the dummy for the pointsman to get clearance from Eastleigh West signal box: this was because the first leg of the triangle was also the entrance to the diesel depot from the Portsmouth line.

After the first leg of the triangle, it was necessary to get down and change a pair of points, but the next pair were sprung points which pushed open as the engine went through.

The 'shed-engine' turn was only an afternoon duty; this involved shunting out the first 5 or 6 roads of the shed. All these engines were 'dead' engines and were there for things like boiler washout, intermediate examinations and light repairs. As soon as work was complete on one, it was shunted out and others requiring attention were shunted in. The last turn was a preparation and disposal turn; we booked on at 6:45p.m. and always prepared three engines and disposed of three.

Most of the work in the ashpan gang was routine but quite interesting. Every afternoon at about 3.30, a 9F 2-10-0 used to come down through the disposal pit to take on extra coal. This engine went right through to the midlands, hence the need to have a full tender. Its duty was a train of full oil tankers, the type we would bring up from Fawley when I was learning the job. This train was routed up the old Great Western line that branched off the mainline at Shawford Junction and went up through Winchester Chesil and Whitchurch. At that time I think Eastleigh men took it as far as Didcot.

On one particular afternoon I happened to know the fireman on this duty quite well. He said "Come with us for the afternoon"; I was very tempted but declined, fearing what would happen if I was found out. When I spoke to Jimmy about it later he said, "Of course you could have gone, we'd have covered for you." So that was it, my only chance to go up that particular line and I blew it!

When as a crew it was necessary to take a big engine around the triangle before stabling it on shed it was always me who did it. The main reason for the use of the triangle was that the turntable was restricted in size: the biggest it would take being a '73' standard. Hence the bigger stuff, 9Fs, 'West Countries', 'Merchant Navies' and

The same engine, No. 689 together with an unidentified S15 by the disposal coal / watering roads.　　　*Mark Abbott*

S15s all had to go round the triangle to turn. My task in this area came about when I first started with Jimmy and because of the problem with his legs. As I mentioned earlier, it was necessary to dismount from the footplate to change the first set of points by hand. Also the trackwork at this point was properly made up on ballast, and as a result it was a long way from the footplate and bottom step to the ground. Similarly Jimmy did not fancy the climb back up again either. I can still hear his Cockney tones to this day, "…'ere mate, take her round the triangle will you, my old legs are playing up today…". So from that first day on I got to take all the big stuff round the triangle. What an experience for a seventeen-year-old lad who until only a few months ago had driven nothing bigger than a pushbike. Of course it was very much against the rules for young firemen to drive like this, but authority turned a blind eye as long as there were not too many mishaps, it was just expected of us and it helped to keep the job going. To be honest, if the fireman hadn't done a lot of the driving, especially on the pits, the job would have ground to a halt.

In my time as a fireman I can only remember one mishap on the triangle, this when a young fireman got too carried away with a 'West Country' class on the second leg of the triangle and couldn't stop in time. He hit the concrete stop block and almost ended up on the runway of Eastleigh airport.

We were never given any instruction on how to drive the engines, because officially we weren't supposed to be driving. If you weren't sure about anything you asked your driver but mostly we just picked it up by watching as we went along.

I was of course even more grateful to Ken for allowing me to do that spot of driving a few months beforehand as it had given me so much more confidence. I must admit for the first few months I felt a bit out of my depth and more than a little nervous. You had to be so careful taking engines around the triangle and into the shed: remember these had stood on the disposal pits for an hour or two before having fireboxes and smokeboxes cleaned, consequently they were all very low on steam pressure, anything between 60Ibs and a 150lbs was all there was. The standard types were fine, they had excellent steam brakes which worked extremely well regardless of steam pressure, but the 'West Countries' and 'Merchant Navies' were a different matter altogether, their brakes were quite useless with such low boiler pressure. Many is the time I have crept into the shed with one of these all set ready to make a dash for the hand brake as you dare not nudge the engine in front in case it was being prepared and had a crew working on it.

THE LAST STEAM AGE FIREMAN PART 2

We also got to drive engines straight out of Eastleigh works after a general overhaul. They would come down through the disposal pit to be fully coaled before going back to their home sheds, and the majority also needed turning. The last Merchant Navy I drove around the triangle before I left the ashpan gang was *Canadian Pacific*, probably having also received its last general overhaul before it was taken out of service.

The shed engine turn could be a slow and tedious affair, we would take any engine that was available on the pits, usually a Midland tank that was not due back out for at least the next eight hours and use it for the afternoon. Nine times out of ten the engines we wanted were way back in the shed. Jimmy would be given a shed plan when he signed on, marked with all the engines we had to move. It also indicated where they had to go, either to another dead road or somewhere else to be lit up. If you wanted an engine that was fourth or fifth back in the shed the procedure was as follows; firstly we buffered up to the first engine and coupled on, then I had to climb on the footplate of this engine, take off the handbrake, check the cylinder drain cocks were open and the reverser was in mid gear. Next it was climb down and wave Jimmy on to the next one and so on until we had coupled up all the engines that needed to be towed out. This could have been up to six or even more engines until we were able to reach the one we wanted.

Coupling up was never easy because it was necessary to stand down in the pit under the engine, with the coupling over your head, far more difficult than doing it at ground level. Towards the end of a busy afternoon it became a real trial of strength, how some of the smaller lads managed I don't know.

Once all the engines were coupled up, we would drag the lot out, including of course the one we wanted. This was then placed where it had to go, after which the whole procedure was repeated but in reverse; back into the shed, uncouple the first one climb on the footplate, handbrake on,

wave Jimmy on a few feet, uncouple the next one, and so on until they were all stabled back in the shed. We would then move on to the next engine needed, hence it was a time-consuming operation. Some days there would only be six or so engines to move, other days it could be three times that number.

I recall on one particular day in the summer we were on 'shed engine' and it was the same old story, one of the engines we wanted was about fourth back in the shed, but the trouble was that it was a very hot and sunny day. On such days it was difficult to see very far into the gloomy interior of the shed whilst standing outside in the bright sun. I always held a 'whitey' or a newspaper in my hand which made it much easier for Jimmy to see my hand signals through the gloom of the shed. We started the usual procedure slowly moving back into the shed and coupling up as we went. We already had a couple of 'dead' engines on the front which meant that, even as we got to the last engine, Jimmy was still outside the shed in the bright sun. As usual I gave him the stop signal as he buffered up to the last engine, but even with the 'whitey' in my hand he failed to see my hand signal and kept on coming.

A few feet beyond the engine we wanted was a '76 standard' with 'NOT TO BE MOVED' boards on. By the time Jimmy realised he should have stopped it was too late, he gave the standard quite a thump which shoved it on at least a foot, unfortunately there was a fitter working on it. To say he was angry was an understatement, he was only a little chap but he gave me the most awful rollicking, questioning my ability as a fireman and even doubting the validity of my parents' marriage, and other things as well! I had to just stand and take it. I did try to explain the situation to him but to no avail. In the end it was our fault, plain and simple, the rule was you never moved an engine with 'NOT TO BE MOVED' boards on. The whole situation could have had disastrous consequences for the fitter and even today, it still makes me shudder to think of it.

'N' No 31859 awaiting its next turn of duty at Eastleigh on 3 March 1964. This engine would survive a further 18 months until September 1964.
Tony Molyneaux

No. 92006 coaled and ready for its next working. In the foreground is mixture of ash, steam coal and ovoids, April 1963.
Tony Molyneaux

Jimmy was quite unaware of the mayhem we had caused, still being outside the shed in the bright sun, when he discovered he was most upset by what had happened. I think a modern day health and safety man would have apoplexy if he saw what we got up to as youngsters back then.

By comparison, some of the preparation and disposal turns were normally quite straight forward. Of the three engines we were expected to attend to, two would be standard types with rocker grates and self-cleaning smoke boxes; in total these only took about ten minutes each to do. The other one was always an S15 which was a different matter altogether. Having a long and narrow nine foot' firebox it presented quite a challenge to a young fireman. The plan was to shovel all the good fire from one side to the other side of the firebox, then with the dart, break up the clinker. With this done the pricker was used to clean the air space between the firebars. Next was to shovel the clinker out with the clinker shovel. When the clinker was out on that side of the box, you shovelled the good fire on to the now clean half of the grate and started to clean the other side of the firebox.

My lasting memory of this is having to beat out the end of the clinker shovel with the coal pick every few minutes, as after moving a few shovels of clinker the end of the shovel would curl up with the heat and become quite useless. It took a lot of practice to handle those twelve foot long fire irons, the main trouble being they just got so hot. Wearing leather gloves helped a bit whilst wrapping a

'brownie' or two around the fire iron also assisted, but even so after a few minutes this would start to smoulder and burn as the heat travelled up the handle. It was a test of skill and almost a work of art to get a loaded clinker shovel out through the fire door and over the side and certainly hard and very hot work, exactly the sort of job that broke a few young firemen's hearts.

Compared with the firebox though, the smoke box was a piece of cake. Preparation was also quite straight forward once you had found all the tools you needed, as mentioned before it could be a real problem trying to find them all. It could easily take more than half of the preparation time, which was just over an hour for most types. We would scour the shed, the dead engines and even engines coming in to the shed to find all the tools needed.

The next problem could be the sand boxes. We always hoped and prayed these did not need much sand to fill them up. Looking from the front of the shed the sand furnace was right down the bottom of the shed on the right hand side. My problem was that I was very conscientious and always felt obliged to fill the sand boxes right up, the sand being carried in a type of metal coal hod and if you had to carry three or four of those from one end of the shed to the other you were on your knees with arms a foot longer than when you started. Carrying was not the only problem, either: once back at the engine these full loads of sand then had to be lifted on to the running board above your head, this

70

was apt to make your knees tremble, especially if it was the fourth one!

The rest of the preparation was easy by comparison after the sandboxes. Check the ashpan and the smokebox and make sure they had been emptied properly and ensure the smokebox had been closed tightly. We had then to clean and fill the three oil lamps and the water gauge lamp, this even if it was daylight, as the chances were that it would be dark before the engine returned to the shed. The fire would have to be spread over the box and the fire made up. At Eastleigh we never made up a big fire causing the engine to blow off, that was always left to the fireman who was taking the engine out. The final job was to clean down the footplate, trim the coal and that was about it. Whilst engaged in the latter, the driver would be doing all the oiling around the engine.

The last engine we prepared on the night turn (sign on at 6.45 pm), was always a 'West Country', 6:18 am off shed the next morning. This was booked to run light engine to Southampton, ready to work the first businessmen's train up to London - the word commuter had not been invented back then. I seem to remember that during the extremely cold winter of 1963, this last engine was prepared ahead of us, as a lot of the businessmen had complained that the train was too cold. (The engine being prepared by a spare crew and taken down to Southampton an hour earlier to steam heat the train!)

After a few months in the ashpan gang I acquired the nickname of Garth, (for the younger reader, Garth was a strong-man in a cartoon strip that ran in the Daily Mirror for many years). Being well over six foot tall and having spent the first year after leaving school working on forestry,

mostly tree felling - it was all axe and crosscut saw work as there were no chain saws in those days - I was as strong and fit as I was ever going to be. It was a senior fireman helping out on the disposal pits one day who gave me this nickname; I must have done something to earn the nickname but cannot for the life of me remember what it was. The interesting thing is how quickly it spread and within a few weeks everyone I knew was using it, even the running foreman.

Around midnight a few weeks later around midnight the running foreman's assistant came down to the pits to find me, saying, "bring your bag and coat, Garth, the running foreman wants you - and be quick". I hurried up to the office to be told there was a freight down at Bevois Valley (Southampton) with no fireman, "...off you go." The depot Bedford van was already outside with the driver waiting and so off we went. Within ten minutes we were at Bevois Valley, I was dropped at the yard entrance and soon found my engine, a '75' standard. I made myself known to the driver who was having a chat to the guard. He said, "We leave in about five minutes for Salisbury, you had better make up the fire". I climbed aboard and had a look in the firebox, there was quite a good fire on but I set to with enthusiasm and soon had the box filled right up, and I mean filled right up.

Came the time to leave, the boiler pressure was just below the red line and we had a full boiler of water, perfect, or so I thought. We got the dummy off which took us to the yard exit signal; this came off as we approached and we were away. Once on the move my first job was to signal to the guard for which I used the water gauge lamp, he returned my signal with his guard's lamp; this was always done to make sure the train was all together.

At 6.45 pm in the early evening of 17 May 1962, No. 76064 heads south past Stoneham sidings.

Tony Molyneaux

Another 76xxx, type, this one No. 76069 seen with a Portsmouth to Cardiff working near Romsey on 10 June 1962.

Tony Molyneaux

I cannot remember the exact load but it was quite modest, we pounded up towards Eastleigh in great style, the boiler pressure on the red line and I naively starting to think how easy this was going to be. As we slowed at Eastleigh to take the left hand line at the junction, the engine started to blow off, so on went the injector again.

Once on the Salisbury branch my driver opened up again and then the troubles started. I could not believe my eyes, the pressure gauge was creeping back at an alarming rate, the driver noticed what was happening and shouted above the din, "...get the pricker down and pull the fire through." As soon as I started to pull the fire through, my problem was there for all to see and of course of my own making. I was pulling back nothing but black unburnt coal. Instead of a roaring red inferno I had a great big black sticky pudding of a fire. In my haste to make a good impression on my driver I had completely forgotten the lessons of six months ago, and as I sweated and heaved on the pricker, the words 'controlled firing' and 'little and often' were racing through my mind. I just could not believe I had been so stupid.

That was also the story of the entire trip to Salisbury, five minutes with the pricker, then on with the injector and back to the pricker but even so we still kept pounding, despite steam pressure back to 120lbs on several occasions. The fact that we were loose coupled helped: if we'd had to maintain a vacuum we would have come to a stand long before. We passed Chandlers Ford and then Romsey. There was a brief respite here when we necessarily slowed for the junction with the Southampton line, but then it was onwards towards Kimbridge and then to Dunbridge.

By the time we had passed the next station at Dean the fire was starting to liven up and there was a slight rise in steam pressure. But that was just a precursor to another problem that was coming my way and I am sure you can guess what that was.

By the time we got to Salisbury I now had a monstrous white hot fire that was making steam hand over fist and would have taken us half way to Exeter. But alas we had to leave our train in the yard at the west end of the station and then go and sit in Salisbury loco' shed for an hour. I was not popular. Between bouts of blowing off I apologised to my driver for my inept performance, saying rather sheepishly, "I think I put too much on". He looked at me in a bit of an old-fashioned way and asked me my status and experience. When I told him "ashpan gang" and "experience none apart from shunting turns" and this was my first trip on the mainline on a tender engine he gave a wry smile and from that point on gave me all the help and advice I could have asked for.

By the time it was time to leave the loco' shed our engine had quietened down and the fire had lost a lot of its heat, but even so there was this big fire in the box. We left the loco shed just as dawn was breaking and ran back through the station to the goods yards at the eastern end of the station ready to back on to our train. With about fifteen minutes before departure my driver advised me to make up the fire, level with the bottom of the fire hole door and to taper it to a few inches under the brick arch, then a few minutes before departure put just half a dozen round the firebox and close the doors. This he said, would probably take us right back to Eastleigh. He watched my every move this time just to make sure I did it right.

Again we had a very modest load of mixed wagons, a typical freight of that time I suppose, and as our departure time arrived I did as I was told, a quick half dozen round the box and closed the doors. Now with a full boiler and the steam pressure gauge on the red line we were off. Once on the move I waved to the guard although this time as it was daylight I just used a cloth, he again acknowledged my wave and all was well.

We roared up through Fisherton Tunnel which had quite a steep gradient and burst out into the daylight just before Tunnel Junction signal box where we took the right-hand line that took us back to Eastleigh, the way we had come earlier - the line straight on was the main line on to London and not our territory. Incidentally my father was a signalman at Tunnel Junction box when I was born, towards the end of the Second World War. Once on the branch proper my driver shut off steam, the gradient was in our favour most of the way back, and apart from the occasional breath of steam we ran all the way back to Eastleigh. Even

so I kept jumping up and looking in the firebox noticing the fire was getting lower and lower. In the end the driver could stand it no longer saying, "For goodness sake sit down and enjoy the ride!"

All I had to do all the way back was put the injector on occasionally. As we ran through Chandlers Ford the steam brake was used to warm up the brake blocks and by the time we got to Eastleigh speed was down to walking pace, signals were off and we drifted across the main lines and came to a stop in the yard the other side of the station, unhooked and ran back to the loco sheds.

Now I was allowed to look inside, he was of course right as well, the fire had burnt right down and was just right to dispose of. So ended my first trip on the main line with a large tender engine. I had made a right pigs-ear of it and made so many mistakes I could not believe it, but they were mistakes I never made again. They say you learn by your mistakes and I certainly did that night, I had a few more rough trips but they were not down to my stupidity.

To be continued

Roger's painting of Tunnel Junction at Salisbury.

SOUTHERN EPHEMERA

WE HAVE RECENTLY BEEN PRIVILEGED TO ACCESS PART OF THE REMARKABLE COLLECTION OF SOUTHERN AND CONSTITUENT PAPERWORK COURTESY OF MICHAEL BROOKS. I AM SURE ALL WILL AGREE THERE ARE EXAMPLES HERE NOT SEEN FOR MANY DECADES.....

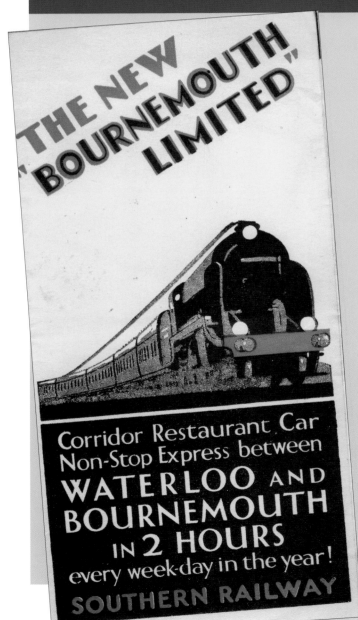

"THE NEW BOURNEMOUTH LIMITED"

Corridor Restaurant Car Non-Stop Express between WATERLOO AND BOURNEMOUTH IN 2 HOURS every week-day in the year!

SOUTHERN RAILWAY

PLYMOUTH, DEVONPORT AND SOUTH WESTERN JUNCTION RAILWAY.
(Bere Alston and Callington Line.)

CHEAP
MARKET TICKETS
TO
Plymouth & Devonport
WILL BE ISSUED
THURSDAYS & SATURDAYS,
AS UNDER :—

	A.M.	A.M.	FARES:
			3rd Class Return from any Station TO
Callington Road	7.23	9.50	
Stoke Climsland	7.32	9.57	Devonport 1/8
Latchley - -	7.39	10.3	Plymouth 1/10
Gunnislake - -	7.51	10.13	(North Rd.)
Calstock - -	8.8	10.28	Plymouth 2/-
			(Friary)

Available for return by any Train on the day of issue only.

Children under Three Years of Age, Free; Three and under Twelve, Half-fares.

The Tickets are not transferable, and are subject to the conditions published in the Company's Time Tables and Bills, and in the General Notice containing the conditions on which Tickets are issued to Passengers. Attention is particularly directed to the conditions limiting the availability of Cheap Tickets.

Passengers travelling without personal luggage with these Cheap Market Tickets may carry with them 60 lbs. of marketing goods free of charge (at their own risk), all excess over that weight will be charged for.

February, 1908.   (By order) **J. W. BURCHELL,** *Secretary.*

BRADBURY, AGNEW, & CO. LD., PRINTERS, LONDON AND TONBRIDGE.   (4211-2-08.)

The new RAILWAY Air Services Ltd.,

in conjunction with the Spartan Air Lines, Ltd., provide the quickest service between London and the Isle of Wight.

Passengers are conveyed by car from Victoria to the Croydon Airport, thence by fast comfortable 3-Engined Air Liners to Ryde in forty minutes, and to Cowes in fifty minutes.

The cabins are well ventilated, free from excessive noise and vibration, and provide ample accommodation for six or seven passengers and their hand luggage.

Magnificent views of the most beautiful parts of Surrey, and Hampshire, including Dorking, Haslemere, Midhurst, Portsmouth and Southsea, Southampton Water, the Solent and South Coast, are obtainable from any seat in the air liner.

The only Air Service by which holders of return tickets may, if they so wish, return First Class by steamer and Southern Railway.

These tickets, therefore, provide, under one charge, the possibility of travelling by Air, Rail, Sea and Road.

LONDON

ISLE OF WIGHT Swift Air Services

DAILY (Sundays included)
May 1st until 31st August
(Revised Time Table will operate Sept. 1st).

FROM LONDON

	a.m.	a.m.	From May 15 p.m.	p.m.
VICTORIA STATION dep. (Airway Terminus)	8 45	11 0	3 30	6 15
CROYDON AIRPORT .. dep.	9 25	11 40	4 10	6 55
RYDE AIRPORT* arr.	10 5	12 20 p.m.	4 50	7 35
COWES .. .. arr. (Somerton Aerodrome)	10 15	12 30	5 0	7 45

TO LONDON

	a.m.	a.m.	From May 15 p.m.	p.m.
COWES .. .. dep. (Somerton Aerodrome)	8 30	10 45	3 15	6 0
RYDE AIRPORT* dep.	8 40	10 55	3 25	6 10
CROYDON AIRPORT .. arr.	9 20	11 35 p.m.	4 5	6 50
VICTORIA STATION arr. (Airway Terminus)	10 0	12 15	4 45	7 30

* Will call at Bembridge Aerodrome if inducement offers and circumstances permit.

Tickets and Reserved Seats must be booked in advance, and can be obtained at the Offices shown overleaf.

Passengers are conveyed by special motor car between Victoria (Airway Terminus) and Croydon Airport, and vice versa.

CROYDON AIRPORT

COWES ► RYDE
Bembridge

ONLY 1½ Hours

LONDON & ISLE OF WIGHT
Via Croydon Aerodrome

By Swift Air Liners
to and from

RYDE AND COWES

Return Tickets also available for return 1st Class by Southern Railway.

30/- Single

50/- Return

Special Luggage in Advance facilities.

Tickets and reserved seats must be booked in advance and can be obtained at

IMPERIAL AIRWAYS LTD.
AIRWAY TERMINUS, VICTORIA STATION.
(Phone : Victoria 2211.)
The Southern Railway Enquiry Offices at :
VICTORIA   WATERLOO
CANNON CROSS   LONDON BRIDGE
CHARING CROSS   HOLBORN VIADUCT
and the following Stations :
Bromley South, Chatham, Chislehurst, East Croydon, Gravesend Cent., Maidstone East, Tunbridge Wells, Sevenoaks (Tubs Hill), Redhill, Wimbledon, Kingston, Sutton, Richmond and Staines.

SPARTAN AIR LINES LTD.
SOMERTON AERODROME, COWES.
(Phone 316.)
BEMBRIDGE AERODROME, BEMBRIDGE. (Phone 15.)
FOUNTAIN GARAGE, LTD., COWES. (Phone 323.)
And the following Southern Railway Isle of Wight Stations :
Ventnor, Shanklin, Sandown, Bembridge, Newport, Ryde Esplanade.

Also from principal Tourist Agencies.

Printed in England by Waterlow and Sons Ltd.

RAILWAY AIR SERVICES

IN CONJUNCTION WITH SPARTAN AIR LINES LTD

CROYDON AIRPORT

LONDON & ISLE OF WIGHT

COWES ► RYDE
Bembridge

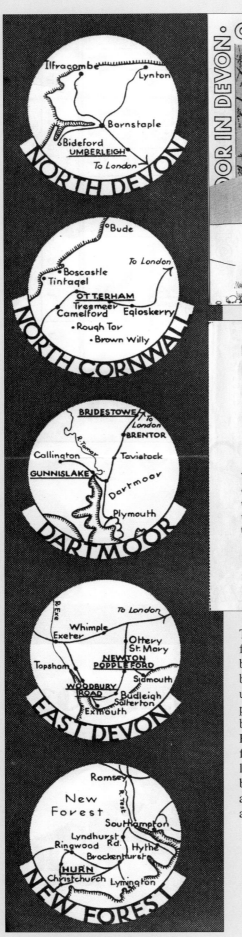

Furnished and fully equipped for a Family or Party of 4 to 6 people

Inclusive Charges per Coach :

50/- per week	70/- per week
April, May, June	July, August, September

These charges include the use of all bed and table linen and a very complete equipment of cutlery and crockery. The only condition is that in addition to the rent, no fewer than 4 "Monthly Return" Tickets to the site where the coaches are berthed are required. You travel by any train and will find everything ready for you. Camping coaches can be booked NOW.

SOUTHERN RAILWAY

Southern Railway Advertising. Ad. 2933/-   Printed by McCorquodale & Co. Ltd., London—29812.

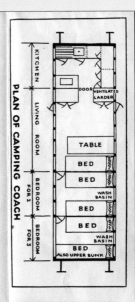

PLAN OF CAMPING COACH

The 'Camping Coach' brochure is stamped for 1935. Produced as an interestingly folder brochure in the style of period it included both a list of locations with these shown underlined on the accompanying maps. One particularly interesting location being Hurn between Ringwood and Christchurch. Perhaps surprisingly the Isle of Wight fails to feature, it would surely have been an ideal location. The plan would also be seemed to be based on a standard 6-wheel vehicle although bogie-coaches were certainly used at a number of sites in later years.

EVENINGS
BY THE SEA

HELEN McKIE

SOUTHERN ELECTRIC

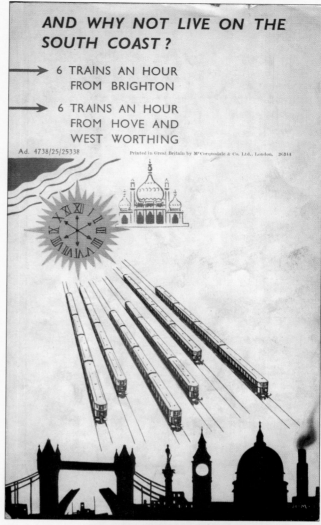

AND WHY NOT LIVE ON THE SOUTH COAST?

→ 6 TRAINS AN HOUR FROM BRIGHTON

→ 6 TRAINS AN HOUR FROM HOVE AND WEST WORTHING

Ad. 4738/25/25338

Printed in Great Britain by McCorquodale & Co. Ltd., London. 36344

One may wonder exactly how many Londoners, both residents and workers were convinced by the publicity. In reality there would probably have been few weeks or even days when it might be said to be a feasible option.

The brochure here was cleverly designed so that upon opening the carriage door the image changed to that of the beach.

DON'T GO STRAIGHT HOME WHEN YOU LEAVE THE OFFICE HAVE A DIP IN THE SEA AND A TASTE OF FRESH AIR

CHEAP TICKETS
EVERY
TUESDAY, WEDNESDAY & THURSDAY

Until October 27th

VICTORIA & LONDON BRIDGE TO		FARE
BRIGHTON	... ...	4/2
HOVE		
PORTSLADE	... ...	4/4
SOUTHWICK		
SHOREHAM	... ...	4/6
LANCING		
WORTHING	... ...	4/9

CHEAP TICKETS also issued from :—

CLAPHAM JUNC., COULSDON SOUTH, EARLSWOOD, EAST CROYDON, HORLEY, MERSTHAM, PURLEY, REDHILL, SALFORDS and THREE BRIDGES

TRAIN TIMES

p.m.

VICTORIA . 6.4, 6.30, 6.35, 7.5

LONDON BRIDGE .. 5.30, 6.5

Return same day by ANY TRAIN

Last services as under :

	p.m. p.m.			p.m.
WORTHING CENTRAL	9.52 10.40	PORTSLADE & WEST		
LANCING	9.45 10.43	HOVE	..	10.41 10.55
SHOREHAM-BY-SEA	10.4 10.47	HOVE	..	10.41 10.57
SOUTHWICK-BY-SEA	10.41 10.50	BRIGHTON	..	10.43 11.10

A—To Salfords, Earlswood, Merstham, Coulsdon South and Purley. B—To Three Bridges, Horley, Redhill, East Croydon, Clapham Jun. and Victoria.

HELEN McKIE

L.S.W.R

NEW ELECTRIC SERVICE

(1st and 3rd CLASS)

— BETWEEN —

WIMBLEDON & WATERLOO

VIA

EAST PUTNEY

All trains for this section lettered **P** as shown above

All trains for this section lettered **P** as shown above

— Commencing —

Monday, 25th October, 1915

and every Weekday thereafter.

THE QUICKEST WAY
Twixt **HOME AND CITY**
COMFORT EN ROUTE

H. A. WALKER   General Manager.

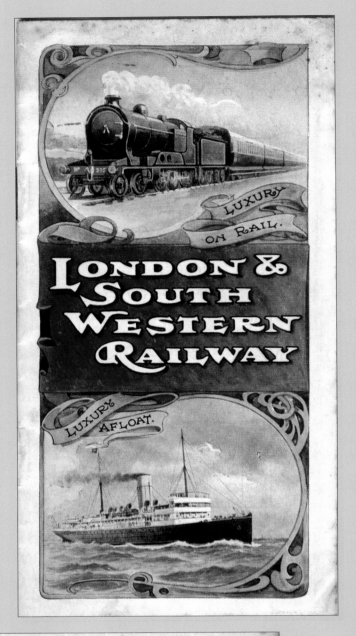

LUXURY ON RAIL.

LONDON & SOUTH WESTERN RAILWAY

LUXURY AFLOAT.

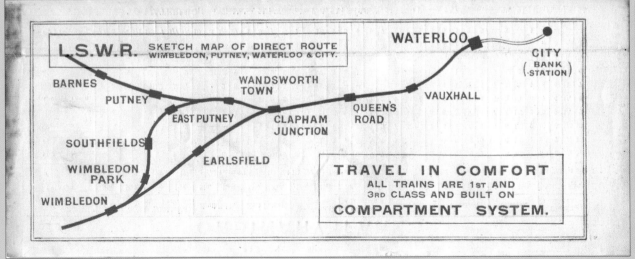

L.S.W.R. SKETCH MAP OF DIRECT ROUTE
WIMBLEDON, PUTNEY, WATERLOO & CITY.

WATERLOO

CITY (BANK STATION)

BARNES

PUTNEY

WANDSWORTH TOWN

VAUXHALL

EAST PUTNEY

QUEEN'S ROAD

CLAPHAM JUNCTION

SOUTHFIELDS

EARLSFIELD

WIMBLEDON PARK

WIMBLEDON

TRAVEL IN COMFORT
ALL TRAINS ARE 1ST AND
3RD CLASS AND BUILT ON
COMPARTMENT SYSTEM.

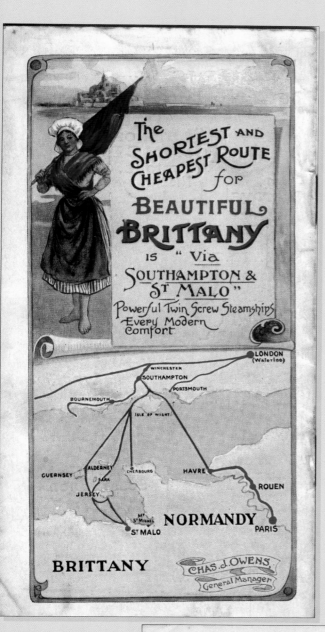

Travel without Trouble.

LUGGAGE IN ADVANCE. To obviate the trouble and anxiety generally occasioned by the care of luggage, the London and South Western Railway Company undertake to collect and deliver in advance the personal luggage of passengers travelling from Waterloo and other London and South Western Stations to the principal health and pleasure resorts.

TICKETS IN ADVANCE. Tickets can be obtained in advance at the London and South Western Company's City and West End Offices, or at the Main Line Booking Office, Waterloo Station.

SEATS RESERVED. A telephone message (Hop 3405) or post-card to Mr. Henry Holmes, Superintendent of the Line, Waterloo Station, London, S.E., will ensure a seat being reserved in the Dining-Saloon or other parts of the Express Corridor Trains between Waterloo and the South and West of England. *No charge is made for the reservation.*

COMPARTMENTS RESERVED. Compartments can also be reserved, upon receipt of previous notice, provided the requisite number of tickets be taken.

PRIVATE SALOON CARRIAGES. Luxurious Saloon Carriages can be provided (by arrangement with the Superintendent of the Line) in the principal Express Trains for the use of family parties, invalids, &c.

THAMES VALLEY RIVERSIDE SEASON.
Frequent Trains from Waterloo to Richmond, Staines, Windsor and Eton, Reading, and other Riverside Stations.

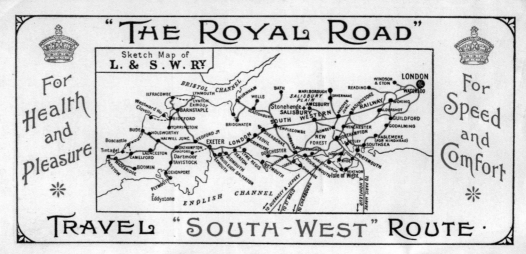

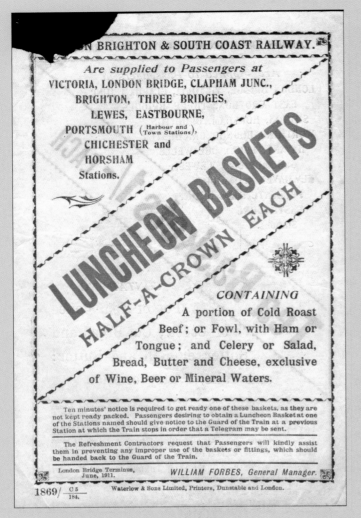

LONDON BRIGHTON & SOUTH COAST RAILWAY.

Are supplied to Passengers at
VICTORIA, LONDON BRIDGE, CLAPHAM JUNC.,
BRIGHTON, THREE BRIDGES,
LEWES, EASTBOURNE,
PORTSMOUTH (Harbour and Town Stations),
CHICHESTER and
HORSHAM
Stations.

LUNCHEON BASKETS
HALF-A-CROWN EACH

CONTAINING
A portion of Cold Roast
Beef; or Fowl, with Ham or
Tongue; and Celery or Salad,
Bread, Butter and Cheese, exclusive
of Wine, Beer or Mineral Waters.

Ten minutes' notice is required to get ready one of these baskets, as they are not kept ready packed. Passengers desiring to obtain a Luncheon Basket at one of the Stations named should give notice to the Guard of the Train at a previous Station at which the Train stops in order that a Telegram may be sent.

The Refreshment Contractors request that Passengers will kindly assist them in preventing any improper use of the baskets or fittings, which should be handed back to the Guard of the Train.

London Bridge Terminus,
June, 1911.   WILLIAM FORBES, General Manager.

1869/ C5/184.   Waterlow & Sons Limited, Printers, Dunstable and London.

LONDON BRIGHTON AND SOUTH COAST RAIL

Are supplied to Passengers at
LONDON BRIDGE, VICTORIA, CLAPHAM JUNC.,
EAST CROYDON, THREE BRIDGES,
SUTTON, HORSHAM, BRIGHTON,
WORTHING, BOGNOR, CHICHESTER,
HAVANT, TUNBRIDGE WELLS,
GROOMBRIDGE, LEWES,
NEWHAVEN HARBOUR,
POLEGATE and
EASTBOURNE
Stations.

Tea Baskets 1/- EACH

CONTAINING
A Pot of Tea, Coffee
or Cocoa; Cut Bread and
Butter or Roll and Butter;
and Cake, Pastry or Bun.

Ten minutes' notice is required to get ready one of these baskets, as they are not kept ready packed. Passengers desiring to obtain a Tea Basket at one of the Stations named should give notice to the Guard of the Train at a previous Station at which the Train stops in order that a Telegram may be sent.

The Refreshment Contractors request that Passengers will kindly assist them in preventing any improper use of the baskets or fittings, which should be handed back to the Guard of the Train.

London Bridge Terminus,
June, 1911.   WILLIAM FORBES, General Manager.

1869/ C5/184.   Waterlow & Sons Limited, Printers, Dunstable and London.

Freshwater, Yarmouth & Newport Railway.

TRAIN STAFF TICKET.   No. 221

DOWN LINE.

Train No._____

TO THE ENGINE-DRIVER.
You are authorised, after seeing the Train Staff for the Section,
to proceed from **CARISBROOKE** to **NINGWOOD**
and the Train Staff will follow.

Date_____

Signed_____

Opposite top - Notwithstanding the use of black paper underneath the original, the thin paper has allowed the reverse side still to appear through. Railway catering is something rarely covered in print, the days when it was indeed possible to partake in style. The change from this to the erstwhile 'BR sandwich' and later style the almost total absence of even a trolley service on most trains is hard to comprehend. Perhaps the time is ripe for a feature on 'Catering on the Southern', any offers.....?

PLYMOUTH, DEVONPORT AND SOUTH WESTERN JUNCTION RAILWAY.
(Bere Alston and Callington Line.)

CHEAP
MARKET TICKETS
TO
Plymouth & Devonport

WILL BE ISSUED

THURSDAYS & SATURDAYS,

AS UNDER :—

	A.M.	A.M.	FARES:
			3rd Class Return from any Station TO
Callington Road	7.23	9.50	
Stoke Climsland	7.32	9.57	Devonport 1/8
Latchley - - -	7.39	10.3	Plymouth 1/10
Gunnislake - -	7.51	10.13	(North Rd.)
Calstock - - -	8.8	10.28	Plymouth 2/-
			(Friary)

Available for return by any Train on the day of issue only.

Children under Three Years of Age, Free; Three and under Twelve, Half-fares.

The Tickets are not transferable, and are subject to the conditions published in the Company's Time Tables and Bills, and in the General Notice containing the conditions on which Tickets are issued to Passengers. Attention is particularly directed to the conditions limiting the availability of Cheap Tickets.

Passengers travelling without personal luggage with these Cheap Market Tickets may carry with them 60 lbs. of marketing goods free of charge (at their own risk), all excess over that weight will be charged for.

February, 1908.   (*By order*) **J. W. BURCHELL**, *Secretary.*

BRADBURY, AGNEW, & CO. LD., PRINTERS, LONDON AND TONBRIDGE. (4211-2-08.)

---

(135)

Freshwater, Yarmouth & Newport Railway.

TRAIN STAFF TICKET.   *No.* 1294

DOWN LINE.

Train No. ....

TO THE ENGINE DRIVER.

You are authorised, after seeing the Train Staff for the Section, to proceed from **NEWPORT** to **CARISBROOKE** *and the Train Staff will follow.*

Date ....

Signed ....

LONDON & SOUTH WESTERN RAILWAY.

INSTRUCTION No. 391.

INSTRUCTIONS TO SIGNALMEN

AS TO

CHANGING DUTY.

Signalmen are hereby instructed in all cases to observe the following Rules in Changing Duties:—

FIRST.—The Men on duty must not give up their duty to other Men when they come into the Box to take to duty until the Signalling operations in hand at the time have first been finally completed:—In other words, the change of duty must not be made while any Signalling or Lever or Instrument working, is, or ought to be, in progress, **and the Sections in all directions have been cleared.**

SECOND.—When more than one Signalman comes on duty to relieve the Men at work in a Box, the new Men must commence duty together and at the same time. For example:—Assuming that two Men have to take the duty over from other two Men, neither of the Men on duty must give up his duty *until both* the new Men are in the Box, and have their coats off, and are both prepared to commence their duties together, and at the same time.

THIRD.—Before giving over their duties, the Men about to leave the Box must give to the Men commencing duty all information necessary to enable the duties to be taken over and carried on with safety.

Every Signalman must Sign the Signal Box Book himself, entering the exact time when coming on or going off duty.

Waterloo Station,
October, 1883.

E. W. VERRINDER.

Waterlow and Sons Limited, Printers, London Wall, London.

WD & SR BUILT WW2 'PILLBOX' BRAKE VANS - A BRIEF HISTORY

David Lindsell

In July, 1941 the Ministry of Supply (MOS) ordered the Southern Railway to construct a batch of twenty "Express Goods Brake Vans" to a current Southern Railway design, Diagram 1579, but with the addition of air brake pipes and two vacuum cylinders which were mounted at one end of the under frame. The MOS ordered another batch of twenty vans in December 1941 to the same design.

The first batch were built at Lancing Works and the second at Ashford Works during the period October, 1941 to March, 1942 and numbered WD 11002 to 11021 / 11022 to 11041 although the original WD numbers allocated to the first four vans were B1 – B4, altered to WD 11002 – 5 in March, 1942. Sixteen vans from the first batch were sent to the Middle East with the first four ending up on various Military Railways in the United Kingdom.

In 1949, two vans came into British Rail ownership via the Shropshire and Montgomeryshire Railway and were numbered M 360327 and M 360328 (believed to be numbers WD 11029 and WD 11037 of the second batch).

(*Source*: "An Illustrated History of Southern Wagons Volume 4" published by Oxford Publishing Company, Mike King and the NRM, York.)

KNOWN DETAILS INCLUDING PRESERVED EXAMPLES
I have produced the following number list, which includes the War Department number, the Southern Railway Private Owner number and the Army number, which was allocated in 1956 plus the BR number where appropriate.

From the first wartime batch.
B3 WD 11004 SR 1011 ARMY 49020.
Currently still with the Army at Bicester numbered WGM 4802.

B1 WD 11002 SR 1009 ARMY 49006
Formerly carried the number WGM 4813. Obtained from Long Marston in dark green livery and currently used by Rocks by Rail (formerly Rutland Railway Museum) as passenger accommodation for rides along one mile of track at Cottesmore, near Oakham, Rutland. In BR fitted van brown livery with fictitious number applied. The van is privately owned.

*B2   WD   11003,   SR   1010,
ARMY 49022*

*Purchased from the Longmoor
Military Railway by the Kent
and East Sussex Railway in
1969, this van was restored in
1974 and again in 1982 when
it carried a fictitious SR
number 56495. Another
overhaul was carried out
during 2006 when it was
painted in BR livery and given
the fictitious number M
360327 which it still carries.
The van is currently in general
use on the railway.*

B4   WD   11005   SR   1012   ARMY   49000. Noted at
Bridgwater, Somerset in 1982. Bought from the Army in
about 1992 by a private owner and based on the Mid-Hants
Railway.   Currently   nearing   completion   of   a   thorough
overhaul at Medstead Wagon Works.

WD 11006 – WD 11021 all went to the Middle East or
North Africa during World War Two

*WD 10022, SR 1013,
ARMY 49011*

*Noted in
Ludgershall yard on
22 July 1991.
Delivered from the
Coventry Railway
Centre in 2009 to
the Chasewater
Railway, Brownhills,
Staffs and privately
owned. Restored in
2010 and now
operating in NCB
blue livery and
numbered 2310.*

WD 11027   SR 1018   ARMY 49015.

*Ex RAF Chilmark in 1995 and
currently preserved at the Yeovil
Railway Centre and in operation
during their Steam Days. In SR livery.*

From the second wartime batch.

WD 11023   SR 1024   ARMY 49017
Residing at Tidworth prior to 1950 and the Shropshire and
Montgomeryshire Railway until closure in 1960, this van
was purchased by the West Somerset Railway from Hessay
322 Engineer Park, York in 1982. It is painted grey with
black under frame and is in use as and when required on the
Railway.

WD 11024   SR 1015   ARMY 49001.
Bought from Long Marston in April 1992 by the Urie
Locomotive Society, originally restored in 2005 in BR

brown livery, the van is operational and is kept at Medstead
on the Mid-Hants Railway.

WD 11025   SR 1016

WD 11026   SR 1017   ARMY 49019
Bridgewater and tendered by BR in July 1979.

WD 11028   SR 1019   ARMY 49002
WD 11029   M 360327
Saw service on the Shropshire and Montgomeryshire
Railway before being taken into BR stock in 1949.

WD 11031   SR 1022   ARMY 49013.

*Noted at the Shropshire and
Montgomeryshire Railway in 1960 and
ex Long Marston in the mid-1980's,
this van is now located on a short
section of track along with a bogie
warflat and palvan at the FIBUA
(fighting in built up areas) site at Liss
in Hampshire.*

WD 11030   SR 1030   ARMY 49012.
Saw service on the Shropshire and Montgomeryshire Railway
and at Tidworth. Bought by the Southern Steam Trust on the
Swanage Railway from MOD at OESD (Ordnance Explosives
Stores Depot), Yardley Chase, Northamptonshire in 1981. It
is operational and painted in BR brown and carries the
fictitious number M 390329.

WD 11032   SR 1023   ARMY 49014.
Saw service on the Shropshire and Montgomeryshire
Railway and at Tidworth. Currently at the Buckinghamshire
Railway Centre, Quainton Road and owned by the Quainton
Railway Society since 20 March 1981. Formerly at Kineton
pre-1977 and bought from the OESD, Yardley Chase,
Northamptonshire. Has recently been repainted in SR livery
and carries the number 1023. Operational.

WD 11033   SR 1024

WD 11034   SR 1025   ARMY 49016
For sale on the March 2011 Tender list and located at
Bicester numbered WGM 4812.

WD 11035   SR 1021   ARMY 49010.
Ex. Longmoor Military Railway and moved to RNAD
Bedenham in 1969, this van was bought by J. J. Smith and
delivered to the Severn Valley Railway on the 10 July 1990.
Parts from SR brake van 55577 used in its restoration
therefore it now carries this fictitious number.

WD 11036   SR 1031

WD 11038   SR 1026   ARMY 49004
Purchased from Devonport Dockyard by three members of
the Plym Valley Railway at Marsh Mills, Plymouth, and
arrived on the railway on the 30 May 1990. The van has
been cut down so that it could work through a low tunnel
between the North and South yards at the Dockyard. Still in
unrestored condition.

WD 11039   SR 1027

WD 11040   SR 1028

WD 11041   SR 1029   ARMY 49007.
Noted at Horton in 1981. This van was another obtained
from stock at OESD, Yardley Chase, Northamptonshire and
bought by the Yorkshire Dales Museum trust based on the
Embsay and Bolton Abbey Railway near Skipton in
Yorkshire. In 2000 it required full replanking and
repainting.

WD 11037   SR 1032   ARMY 49018
M 360328.

Worked on the Shropshire and
Montgomeryshire Railway, then in May
1949 was bought by British Railways
from the MOS for service on the London
Midland Region. At some stage it was
returned to the MOD at Bicester. The van
was purchased by two Bluebell Railway
supporters from RAF Chilmark in August
1991 and delivered by road to the
railway. The van was painted in SR
colours and entered service and has seen
regular use on the Imberhorne tip spoil
trains ever since. It is now located on the
Ardingly branch spur at Horsted Keynes
and is in need of a thorough overhaul.

EXTRACTS FROM THE SOUTHERN RAILWAY TRAFFIC CONFERENCE MINUTES
Compiled by David Monk-Steel

Monday 22nd June 1936.

SOUTHAMPT0N TERMINUS, 16th MAY 1936.

At 2.5 p.m. on the 16th May, an engine was derailed at No.45 crossover road points at Southampton Terminus, causing an obstruction to the up local line and blocking the connections from Nos. 3, 4, 5, and 6 platforms.

The breakdown appliances were ordered from Eastleigh at 2.15 and arrived at 3.20 p.m. rerailment being effected at 4.3 and the line cleared at 4.30 p.m.

Single line working was instituted over the down local line between Chapel Road Crossing and Southampton Terminus for the passage of the 3.22 p.m. special train from Southampton Terminus to Millbrook Dock entrance, which was standing in No. 5 platform road. All other trains were dealt with in Nos. I and 2 platforms and travelled via No. 1 up siding between Southampton Terminus and Chapel Road Crossing. Seven trains sustained delays of from 5 to 27 minutes.

Empty stock to form the 2.57 p.m. and 3.22 p.m. special trains with school parties from Southampton Terminus to Millbrook Dock Entrance had been propelled into No. 4 and 5 platform roads by two engines in each case. The engines required to shunt forward to the up Loco. sidings for engine requirements, and the engines in No. 4 road, owing to the length of the train, were standing beyond the platform starting signal. It was intended that the engines on the train in No. 5 road. should first be shunted and the signalman set points Nos. 45 (down local to up local) and 59 (up local to Loco siding), and operated ground signals Nos. 82 (from No. 5 road) and 74 (up local to Loco. siding at No.59 points).

Driver Horwood on the leading engine in No. 4 road, on seeing No.74 signal go to the "off" position, assumed it was for him and moved forward. He realised his mistake when passing over the trailing end of No.45 points which were run through, and, after stopping, commenced to set back, with the result that one pair of the engine driving wheels became derailed.

The Drivers of the two engines in No. 4 platform road had previously been instructed by the Signalman not to move as he was not ready to deal with them.

Driver Horwood of the leading engine and Driver Hollands of the second engine have been reprimanded.

BETWEEN SOLE STREET and ROCHESTER, 20th MAY, 1936.

At 1.35 p.m. on the 20th May, engine No. 1453, which was running light (tender leading) from Swanley to Gillingham, collided with a permanent way trolley on the down line between Sole Street and Rochester The trolley was smashed and some damage was caused to the tender and engine. There were no personal injuries and no delays to passenger traffic.

At 1.10 p.m. Ganger Pearson telephoned to Signalman Slackford, Rochester Bridge Junction Signal Box, from the instrument fitted to A.59 up line signal, stating that he intended to place a trolley on the up line after the passing of the 11.18 a.m. train from Ramsgate and that later he would transfer the trolley to the down line.

Pearson then telephoned to Signalman Marriott at Sole Street Signal Box giving the same information and a reply was received that the only traffic on the down line would be the 12.26 p.m. and 2.10 p.m. trains from Victoria. Marriott states he was under the impression that Pearson was speaking from Rochester Bridge Junction.

Pearson then sent a man back along the up line to act as Hand Signalman, and after the 11.18 am, train from Ramsgate had passed at 1.20 p.m. the trolley was placed on the up line. The vehicle was propelled by Pearson and four Lengthmen from Signal A.59 to a point about thirty yards short of Cuxton Road Signal Box, which was switched out of circuit at the time. The trolley was not loaded, and, therefore, did not cause the indicators in Sole Street Signal Box to show "Track occupied."

At about 1.15 p.m. Signalman Marriott at Sole Street was advised that a light engine was to run from Swanley to Gillingham following the12.26 p.m. train from Victoria. This train passed the Signal Box at 1.20 p.m. and went by Ganger Pearson at 1.25 p.m.

At 1.27 p.m. Marriott telephoned to Signalman Slackford at Rochester Bridge Junction advising him of the running of the light engine and asked whether Ganger Pearson was there as be wished to warn him also. Slackford replied that Pearson was already engaged in trolleying. The light engine passed Sole Street Signal Box at 1.30 p.m., at which time the trolley was transferred from the up to the down line.

Lengthman Hollands had followed the trolley along the up line in the direction of Cuxton Road and at 1.32 p.m., when he reached Signal C.R.4, about 250 yards from the gang, he telephoned to Sole Street advising Marriott that the trolley was then on the down line. Marriott told him that a light engine had left Sole Street and must then be close to Cuxton Road.'

Ganger Pearson and his four men had already started to load the trolley with sleepers, and they did not hear or see the engine until it was near them. The down line approaching Cuxton Road falls steeply and is on a sharp left hand curve, and, as the engine was running tender first, the Enginemen could not see the trolley until closely approaching it The speed of the engine at the time of the impact is estimated at 35-40 miles per hour and the trolley became wedged in the under gear of the tender, fourteen minutes elapsing before the debris could be cleared.

A joint enquiry was held and the Officers concluded that Signal man Marriott was to blame for not obtaining a clear understanding with Ganger Pearson as to the point from which the latter telephoned. Marriott also failed to observe the additional instruction to Rule 215 on Page 2 of Supplement No. 1 to the General Appendix as he should have stopped the light engine and warned the Driver of the possibility of a trolley being on the down line ahead.

The collision was, however, the direct result of the failure of Ganger Pearson to observe the provisions of Rule 215 (d) i.e. to send out a Hand Signalman to the requisite distance to protect the trolley before it was placed on the down line. Pearson frankly admitted his omission and the primary responsibility for the irregularity rests with him.

Ganger Pearson has been suspended from duty for three days and Signalman Marriott has been cautioned.

WATERLOO, 26th MAY.

At 5.51 p.m. on the 26th May, the 4.10 p.m. special boat train from Southampton Docks to Waterloo, conveying passengers from the "Empress of Britain", came into sharp contact with the hydraulic buffer stops of No. 13 platform road at Waterloo, the buffers being driven in about 4 ft. Eight passengers and the Guard complained of injury or shock,

Extensive damage was caused to crockery in the Pullman car formed in the train. An automatic coupling and four electric lamp shades were also broken.

Guard Bedford states that the train entered the station under proper control and that the Driver appeared to be making a normal stop.

Driver Cannock states that he had occasion to release the brake to reach the end of the platform, but misjudged the distance and weight of the train, which consisted of 14 vehicles. Cannock has been suspended front duty for two days.

VICTORIA, 4th JUNE

At 7.34 p.m. on the 4th June, when the 4.46 p.m. train from Portsmouth Harbour to Victoria was entering No. 17 platform at the latter Station, an axle broke on the rear bogie of Pullman Car No. 11, causing the vehicle to be derailed. One passenger complained of shock.

The up main line from Battersea Pier to Victoria was blocked until 8. 1 p.m., whilst an examination was being made, and this, coupled with the fact that Nos. 16 - 17 platform roads ware out of use, resulted in traffic being disorganised, the heaviest delay being one of twenty - six minutes to the 7.11 p.m. train from Epson to Victoria, which was following the Portsmouth train on the up main line.

Assistance was requisitioned from Stewarts Lane at 8.25 p.m. and arrived at 9.23, rerailment being effected at 2.26 a.m. the following day. No. 16 platform road was occupied during the rerailing operations, and No.17 platform road was available for use with the commencement of traffic on the following morning, but the signalling connections were not finally restored until 9.30 a.m.

Inspector Adorns, who was on duty in the South Signal Box at Victoria, noticed something amiss with the rear bogie of the Pullman Car as the train passed, and he endeavoured to attract the attention of the train crew by shouting, but was unsuccessful.

Driver Kimber states he made the usual brake applications when approaching the station and the speed was normal, but, when nearing the platform, he observed that the train appeared to be pulling heavily despite the fact that only three or four inches of vacuum had been destroyed. On looking back, he observed the Pullman Car to be running abnormally, and, on attempting to make an emergency brake application, found the whole of the vacuum had, at that moment, been destroyed, bringing the train to a stand in the south section with the rear vehicle opposite the platform ramp.

On examination, it was found that the leading axle of the rear bogie of the Pullman Car had collapsed and that considerable damage had ensued to the permanent way and signal connections in the Yard, From marks subsequently found on ths permanent way and apparatus, it is evident that the initial fracture, together with the resultant derailment and short circuiting of the traction current, had taken place immediately after the Car had negotiated the slip crossing (Nos. 17 and 18 points) which leads from the up main line to "D" Section. At this point, the axle broke asunder at the off side wheel-boss, and while the off side wheel remained with the bogie frame, the axle and nearside wheel came adrift and were carried along under the train until a second breakage occurred at the opposite wheel boss, the axle stem being found on the permanent way near the platform ramp and the nearside wheel under the fifth coach from the engine.

Considerable damage was caused to the undergear of the two vehicles immediately behind the Pullman Car, and a large hole was found to have been cut in the flexible hose connection between the Pullman Car and the following vehicle. This was evidently caused by one of the components which came adrift and resulted in the total loss of vacuum and consequent stopping of the train in the south section when the Driver was about to make an emergency brake application.
A joint enquiry was held and the Officers reported that the breakage of the axle was due to a crack at the inside end of the wheel set flush with the inside face of the off-side wheel boss, which defect could not have been detected in the course of ordinary examination and maintenance.

The broken material will be subjected to expert analysis in the Company's Laboratory.

9610. EPSOM RACE TRAFFIC.

SUBMITTED- Statement of Passenger Traffic in connection with the Epsom Summer Race Meeting, 1936, compared with the year 1935:-

	Number of Tickets collected at Epsom Stations.			
	1936	1935	Increase	Decrease
1st day	9,318	9,723	-	405
2nd "	62,408	42,381	10,027	-
3rd "	9,287	11,350	-	2,063
4th "	13,630	8,676	4,954	-
Totals.	84,643	72,130	12,513	-

Weather in 1935 unfavourable.

Note. On the Sunday previous to the meeting a total of 23,339 passengers visited Epsom, re presenting an increase of 1,181 passengers over 1935.

9611. ASCOT RACE TRAFFIC.

SUBMITTED- Statement of Passenger Traffic in connection with the Ascot Race Meeting, 1936, compared with the year 1935:-

	COMPARATIVE BOOKINGS AND TRAINS FROM WATERLOO.			
	No. of Bookings.		No. of down Trains.	
	1936	1935	1936	1935
1st day	4,701	4,399	28	30
2nd "	6,410	5,489	35	33
3rd "	5,220	5,883	32	34
4th "	3,734	3,594	28	30
Totals.	20,066	19,365	123	127

1936, Thames Valley 'Bus strike,

	NUMBER OF TICKETS COLLECTED AT WATERLOO, BRACKNELL AND ASCOT STATIONS.			
	1936	1935	Increase	Decrease
1st day	9,792	8,453	1,339	-
2nd "	17,229	14,089	3,140	-
3rd "	11,870	11,917	-	47
4th "	8.111	7,114	997	-
Totals.	47,002	41,573	5,429	-

9612. ALDERSHOT. MILITARY TATTOO TRAFFIC.

The following are particulars of the traffic conveyed from and to London and other places in connection with the Aldershot Military Tattoo compared with 1935: -

	No. of Passengers.			
	1936.	1935.	Increase.	Decrease.
Wednesday, June 10th.	1,906	623	1,283	
Thursday, 11th.	1,444	8,378	_	934
Friday, 12th.	2,264	1,914	350	_
Saturday, 13th.	43,654	35,508	8,146	_
Tuesday, 16th.	3,432	2,679	753	_
Wednesday, 17th.	17,476	13,760.	3,716	_
Thursday, 18th.	10,421	8,911	1.510	_
Friday, 19th.	6,043	5,665	378	_
Saturday, 20th.	31,254	25,847	5,407	-
Totals	117,894	97,285	20,609	-

Includes 7,210 passengers travelling by ordinary trains to stations in the Tattoo area. These figures not shewn for 1935.
Note. In addition to the above 4,897 passengers, as compared with 7,742 last year, were conveyed to and from the Daylight rehearsal held on Tuesday, 9th June, 1936.

9619. RE-NAMING OF GATWICK STATION.

The Traffic Manager reported that the renaming of Tinsley Green Station as "Gatwick Airport" is likely to cause confusion with the adjoining Race Station, which is known as "Gatwick". It is recommended, therefore, that the latter station be re-named "Gatwick Racecourse" and the name boards and lamp tablets altered accordingly.

9623. NEW WORKS.

The following new works are recommended:-

Station etc.	Nature of Work.	No. of Plan.	Estimated Cost.
Addlestone	Removal of 5-ton yard crane and provision of new 7 ton crane	10/2272	£604
Ashford (Middlesex)	Removal of 5-tons yard crane and provision of new 7 ton crane	10/2266	£586
Between Exeter, Barnstaple and Ilfracombe	Additional service telephone facilities	E. 655/4	£420
London Bridge and Waterloo (Eastern Section)	Improved accommodation for Season Ticket and Enquiry Staff	10/2264 A/P.25	£543
	Conversion of Towel Distributing Depot into Guard's Control Office, and provision of new 'Towel Depot' in 'Cloak Room' Arch.		
Midhurst	Removal of 10-ton yard crane and provision of new 7 ton crane	9/M.31	£655
Cranleigh.	Replacement of 5-ton yard crane and replacement by 7 ton crane	10/22 71 ,K/S	£610
Northam.	Conversion of 10-ton runway to travelling Goliath crane	10/2267	£1,437

THE CANNON STRET SIGNAL BOX FIRE
Friday 5 April 1957

See notes and further images overleaf

Opposite and right - Operations at Cannon Street were severely disrupted on 5 April 1957 when what was later reported as a probable short-circuit in the wiring created a fire which severely damaged the signal box. (When the fire brigade attended and despite the River Thames flowing underneath there was insufficient pressure to lift the water to the required height.) Hand-signalling and pointsmen were in use initially before a temporary solution was in place. This temporary 'signal box' could only control trains in and out without the provision for the use of the engine-release crossovers. In consequence it was necessary to form trains from as much multiple-unit stock as possible which also led to an earlier than planned introduction of the new Hastings DEMU sets into service. (It is believed the idea for this type of ''temporary'' signal came as a result of inspections of the German railway system post WW2. A fleet of this type of vehicle had been available which enabled a rapid resumption of working notwithstanding previous allied bombing.) *Viv Orchard*

THE CANNON STRET SIGNAL BOX FIRE

From notes by Viv Orchard and also the 'Railway Observer' of May 1957

After years of experimenting with double-decker trains and a considerable time and amount of money spent in track, signalling and station alterations, it at last seemed that some alleviation to the serious rush-hour overcrowding on the Southern Region Eastern Section had been achieved by the running of ten-car trains from Cannon Street as from 4th March. But a month later, during the early hours of Friday, 5 April 1957, fire broke out in the relay room of Cannon Street Station signal box. Within half an hour the box, a wooden structure, was wrecked, one end being completely gutted. The signalling and telecommunications system was put out of action completely. After the fire it was stated that a new 140-lever box would not be ready until December; later in the day a 47-lever Westinghouse frame was despatched from Crewe on a special train and, after the necessary alterations will be installed in the northern end of the old box. This will be ready early in May.

At the time of writing, late April, the limited service of electric trains working into Cannon Street is controlled by a system of "three-aspect" hand signalling, utilising red, yellow and green flags. An old brake van, M730181, is parked on the engine spur at the end of platforms 5 and 6, adorned with a Cannon Street destination board and the words "temporary signal box" ; this vehicle is in telephonic communication with Borough Market Junction box and platforms one to five of Cannon Street Station. All incoming trains are halted at the outer home signals where motormen are told which platforms they will use. Signals have been wired to show a red aspect.

The old box had a 143-lever frame of all-electric type installed by Westinghouse in 1926, when the entire approach layout of Cannon Street was altered in connection with the suburban electrification.

A new box will be built on the London Bridge side of the bridge and work has already started on this by pulling down the remains of the old roundhouse next to the sub-station.

The effect of the fire on train services was, of course, immediate and disastrous; of more than 200 trains, most of them suburban electric, which use Cannon Street on a weekday, only a handful could be dealt with. These were all steam, as the electric power was cut off, and they were hand signalled into platforms 1 and 2. Many electric services were cancelled and those which did run were either diverted to Holborn or Victoria, or turned at London Bridge. A number of trains reached Blackfriars and Holborn by way of London Bridge and Metropolitan Junction, the first time this has happened in the up direction for some years. The Bromley North, Hayes and Addiscombe branches were worked as shuttle services. London Transport put on a special emergency bus service, but the opinion was that it was just as quick to walk!

The first steam train diverted from Cannon Street to Victoria was the 6.6 a.m. ex-Ramsgate on 5 April which was hauled by No. 34083 and was due in at 8.30 a.m. There was one other up train diverted that day. Chaos continued to reign throughout the day, and in the evening rush hour up to forty-five minutes were taken by trains between London Bridge and Charing Cross. Of the Cannon Street steam services, the 4.32 Ramsgate and 5.40 Dover were cancelled, and the 5.15 Ramsgate was started from Victoria and called at Chatham as did the 4.45 p.m. departure. The 5.21 p.m. to Faversham started from Rochester and the 6.23 p.m. to Dover from Victoria. The 6.16 p.m. ex-Cannon Street ran seven minutes later with stops at Chatham and Faversham.

On the following day, Saturday, the only passenger trains to use Cannon Street were again steam. During the afternoon electric power was restored and an empty suburban train which had been marooned on a siding was driven away to Slade Green depot. Shuttle services continued to operate on the Bromley, Addiscombe and Sanderstead branches (except for a few peak hour journeys) and Tattenham/Caterham and Gilling-ham/Maidstone trains were all turned at London Bridge (Low Level).

By this time coaching stock rosters were in a hopeless tangle ; much of the Eastern section's quota of EPB stock had disappeared and been replaced by a motley collection of older SUB stock and an 8-HAL formation was twice seen on the Hayes branch.

The much less intensive Sunday service, on 7 April, bore some semblance of normality; practically all scheduled services ran, the Cannon Street trains turning at London Bridge or Charing Cross; a through service to Bromley North was resumed.

On Monday, 8 April the first interim emergency timetable was put into force. The main effect of this was to transfer nearly all rush hour Charing Cross and Cannon Street steam trains to Victoria. To provide paths for these, eight up and ten down Holborn/Blackfriars suburban electrics were cancelled, also one from Victoria. Some Central Section services which normally use the Eastern side of Victoria were run from the Brighton side and three South London line trains turned at Battersea Park to enable this to be done. The up "Night Ferry" was re-timed to arrive twenty-eight minutes later.

Of those Cannon Street steam services not transferred to Victoria, the 5.50 a.m. Dover starts from Holborn Viaduct at 5.40 a.m., the 6.22 a.m. to Dover and 7.0 a.m. to Ramsgate from Charing Cross at 6.17 and 6.53 a.m. respectively, the 4.32 p.m. Ramsgate from Rochester, the

Above and interior opposite - *The replacement 'box on the other side of the river, this opened from 15 December 1957 and utilising a Westinghouse frame from the London Midland Region. The frame and structure were larger than necessary for just Cannon Street as it was intended that the new box take over the work of Borough Market and Metropolitan Junctions. In the event this never occurred and many of the levers in the new 'box were spare. It is possible when the structure was demolished in 1976, part of the the frame may have gone to Clapham Junction Training School. It is thought the whole is now in the hands of the Isle of Wight Steam Railway although part may be with Malden Miniature Railway at Hampton Court Junction. Oddly, Westinghouse have no knowledge of it!*

4.38 p.m. Folkestone from Sevenoaks and the 6.23 p.m. Dover from Rochester. Some mid-day Charing Cross-Hastings trains are turned at London Bridge (Low Level). To summarise the position, the following trains have been cancelled : 12.18 p.m. (S.O.) ex-Cannon Street; 7.35 a.m. ex-Ramsgate. The following trains from Charing Cross now leave from Victoria : 8.25 a.m., 9.15 a.m., 9.25 a.m., 12.16 p.m. (S.O.), 12.55 p.m. (S.O.), 1.15 p.m. (S.O.), 1.25 p.m. (S.X.), and 6.22 p.m. (S.X.).

The following trains from Charing Cross now leave from London Bridge : 11.54 a.m. (S.O.), 2.25 p.m. (S.X.), 3.25 p.m. (S.X.), 5.25 p.m. (S.O.) and 7.35 p.m. (S.O.). The following trains start from Rochester :4.32 p.m. (S.X.), 5.21 p.m. (S.X.) and 6.23 p.m. (S.X.) all formerly from Cannon Street. The 1.15 p.m. (S.O.) ex-Cannon Street commences at

Chatham ; the 4.35 p.m. (S.O.) ex-Charing Cross and the 4.38 p.m. and 6.18 p.m. ex-Cannon Street start from Sevenoaks, whilst the 5.29 p.m. ex-Charing Cross and 5.40 p.m. ex-Cannon Street have been combined and leave Victoria at 5.30 p.m. with a connection at Tonbridge. All other down Cannon Street trains use Victoria..

Of the up trains the 7.24 a.m. (S.X.) ex-Ashford terminates at Sevenoaks with an electric train connection for Victoria ; the 8.20 a.m. (S.X.) ex-Herne Bay commences at Ramsgate at 7.35 a.m. and the 1.10 a.m. (S.X.) ex-Hastings is extended from Ton-bridge to Victoria. In addition to up morning rush-hour trains the following have been diverted to Victoria : 9.40 a.m. (S.O.) ex-Margate, 10.10 a.m. (S.O.) ex-Hastings, 11.10 a.m. (S.O.) ex-Hastings, 11.30 a.m. (S.X.) ex-Ramsgate, 3.20 a.m. (S.X.) ex-Hastings and 4.10 p.m. (S.X.)

On Monday, 8 April the trains from the Chatham line fared better than those from Sevenoaks. The Hastings trains were particularly unfortunate and got out of course. As the first week wore on matters improved ; the signalmen got used to operations and the Hastings trains improved (possibly Hastings crews are not very conversant with the Bickley-Victoria section).

The second week of operation opened much the same as the first, presumably a new shift had to settle down. 16 April was an unhappy day, but on Maundy Thursday a relief boat train was sandwiched in between the 5.53 p.m. to Maidstone and 6.0 p.m. to Hastings and all got through to Bromley remarkably well, there being no noticeable delay. The French 48-hour rail strike did not affect the boat services, with the exception of the "Night Ferry," so this brought little easement of the situation.

The clearance of rush-hour steam services from Charing Cross, referred to earlier, allowed extra electric trains to be run there and permitted the maximum use of Cannon Street possible in the circumstances ; the total Cannon Street service comprised 63 trains, at a rate of three an hour in slack hours and six-seven an hour during the peak

period. The last train out on Monday, 8 April was at 7.16 p.m., a few minutes before dusk. Although later trains might reasonably be expected to run as daylight hours lengthen, none has materialised at the time of writing.

Modifications to the emergency timetable were introduced on Monday, 15 April, the main effect of these being to step up the total number of trains using Cannon Street to 77 up and 78 down. By this time repairs to the damaged box preparatory to installing the temporary frame were well under way, the gutted part having been removed and a new end wall erected. The temporary frame will provide normal signalling for five of Cannon Street's eight platforms, and will enable something like the full electric service to be restored. Steam traction will still be banned, however, since the temporary box will control running signals only and shunt signals will remain out of use; Cannon Street steam services therefore will, in the main, continue to use Victoria, but it is hoped that most if not all, of the Charing Cross main-line trains will revert to their rightful station. It has been suggested that main-line diesel units may be brought into use before the summer service, in order to restore a service from the Hastings line into Cannon Street without involving the use of locomotives.

LONG LIVE THE 'L & B'!

YEO No. E759, with 'E' prefix, modified footplate valance and rerouted vacuum pipe.

As time passes new material on the L & B becomes ever more difficult to locate. Finding not one but at least three new sources is probably quite unusual. With material from the collections of F E Box, Richard Halton, R L Knight, Leslie Walker, and E E Wallis plus ephemera from Michael Brooks, we are delighted to present a few pages of pure nostalgia. Readers may also be interest to learn a little more of the background to the Leslie Walker material, "This set comprises of railway photographs scanned from an album. The album was given to my parents by a boyhood friend's parents. His name was Brian Perkes, and although I knew that he, like myself, had an interest in steam trains, I did not know him very well. He died young as a result of poor health. I remember him as being about 10 years older than myself and initially assumed that he had taken the photographs in the album. I originally dated them as circa 1940, but as a result of comments and dialogue with Flickr members, it seems that the shots may have been taken earlier and I have changed them to circa 1930 instead."

"The album was obviously produced with care. It is comprised of actual photographs, not cuttings out of magazines. Also, it seems highly likely that the author was responsible for all the shots judging by the similarity of presentation throughout the album."

EXE No. E760, with 'E' prefix, no condenser on cab front and no steam heating. It is not known what is in the sack!

Leslie Walker photos (this page).

This remarkable set of images show the L&BR in c.1930. Engines have 'E' prefixes and all are in new Maunsell Olive Green livery.

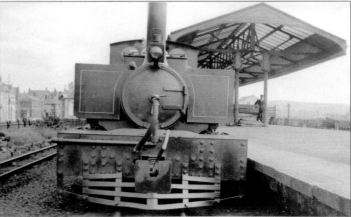

LEW No. E188, with buffer beam numbers painted out and no steam heating. Modified front vacuum pipe following pony truck modifications of 1929.

**Barnstaple
Town 1920s (HJ
Pinn).**

*This photo of
Barnstaple Town
dates from circa
1928.
Locomotive No.
188 LEW
is in original
paint with buffer
beam numbers.
The Manning,
Wardle behind is
still in L&B
livery, whilst
behind that is a
1927 Howard
van with 'X'
bracing. The
wicker
basket on the
engine footplate
appears to
contain coal.*

Locomotive No. 759 YEO leaves Chelfham Viaduct bound for Barnstaple. Locomotives always ran bunker first when returning from Lynton.

Stock lined up awaiting auction at Pilton Yard. The photo was taken on 8th November, with the auction being held on the 13th.

Staff pose at Lynton Station, 25th September 1935. The addition of steam heating equipment to the engines in 1932 necessitated alteration of the vacuum brake piping resulting in a somewhat untidy appearance. The passengers no doubt appreciated the warmth it provided.

Lynton Station 1935.

(Don't forget Stephen Phillips' book, few who have picked it up have found it easy to resist.)

Lynton and Barnstaple Railway.

During JULY, AUGUST & SEPTEMBER, 1907,
Every Tuesday, Thursday & Friday,

DAY EXCURSION TICKETS

Will be issued as under FROM

LYNTON - 8.55 & 10.45 a.m.   BLACKMOOR 9.35 & 11.25 a.m.
WOODY BAY 9.16 & 11.6 a.m.   BRATTON - 9.53 & 11.43 a.m.
CHELFHAM - 10.7 and 11.58 a.m.

Stations to which Tickets are Issued	Return Fares, Third Class.					Return from L. & S.W.R. Stns. Every Tuesday, Thursday and Friday.		
	From LYNTON.	From WOODY BAY	From BLACKMOOR	From BRATTON	From CHELFHAM.	p. m.	p. m.	p. m.
	s. d.	s. d.	s. d.	s. d.	s. d.	3 39	5a19	6b39
BRAUNTON	3 0	2 6	2 0	1 6	1 1	3 26	5 a 6	6b26
MORTEHOE (For Woolacombe Sands)	4 0	3 6	3 0	2 6	2 1	3 15	4a55	6b15
ILFRACOMBE	4 0	3 6	3 0	2 6	2 1	3 2	5a28	6b13
INSTOW	3 0	2 6	2 0	1 6	1 7	2 55	5a22	6b7
BIDEFORD	3 6	3 0	2 6	2 0	1 7	2 55	5a22	6b7
*WESTWARD HO! (Via Bideford)	4 0	3 6	3 0	2 6	2 1	2 45	5a10	From Bideford 5b55
TORRINGTON								Leave Clovelly by Coach
CLOVELLY (Via Bideford & Coach)	7 0	6 6	6 0	5 6	5 1	...	...	4b0

a—These times apply to Tuesdays and Fridays only.
b—These times apply to Thursdays only.

* Tickets are available from Bideford by Bideford and Westward Ho! Railway, or by any of Messrs. Dymond & Son's Road Conveyances.

During JULY, AUGUST & SEPTEMBER,

CHEAP WEEK-END TICKETS

Will be issued to the following Stations:—
FROM LYNTON & BARNSTAPLE RAILWAY STATIONS.

Stations to which Tickets are Issued.	Return Fares, Third Class.					Issue of Tickets and Return.
	From LYNTON	From WOODY BAY	From BLACKMOOR	From BRATTON	From CHELFHAM	
	s. d.	s. d.	s. d.	s. d.	s. d.	
BARNSTAPLE TOWN	2 6	2 0	1 6	1 0	0 7	
MORTEHOE	4 6	4 0	3 6	3 0	2 7	
ILFRACOMBE	4 6	4 0	3 6	3 0	2 7	
INSTOW	3 2	2 8	2 2	1 8	1 3	
BIDEFORD	3 6	3 0	2 6	2 0	1 7	
CLOVELLY (Via Bideford & Coach	7 0	6 6	6 0	5 6	5 1	
TORRINGTON	4 0	3 6	3 0	2 6	2 1	
OKEHAMPTON	7 6	7 0	6 6	6 0	5 7	
BUDE	10 6	9 9	9 3	8 9	8 4	
PLYMOUTH	10 6	10 0	9 6	9 0	8 7	
DEVONPORT	10 6	10 0	9 6	9 0	8 7	
EXETER	7 0	6 6	6 0	5 6	5 1	
EXMOUTH (Via Exeter)	7 9	7 3	6 9	6 3	5 10	

PILTON BRIDGE, BARNSTAPLE.—(2/1530)   CHARLES E. DREWETT, General Manager.

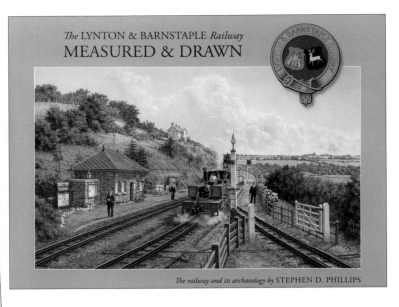

The LYNTON & BARNSTAPLE *Railway*
MEASURED & DRAWN

The railway and its archaeology by STEPHEN D. PHILLIPS

Lynton Station 1934. The locomotive is No. 188 LEW. The box on the left is part of the platform weighing machine apparatus.

A scrapping train hauled by Manning, Wardle No. 759 YEO (Lot 7) and goods brake van No. 56041 (ex-No. 23 built in 1908) (Lot 33) stand at the transhipment siding in Barnstaple with a load of sleepers. By the end of November 1935 YEO had been cut up for scrap, but the wooden body and underframe of van 23 survived in a field in Georgeham, North Devon and can now be seen on display at Woody Bay station.

One of two cranes purchased by the S.R. from George Cohen in 1926. These ex-World War 1 cranes were built by Chambers, Scott of Motherwell and were mounted on French Pechot 60cm gauge bogies. They were probably used to lift artillery shells and at the end of the war they became surplus. They were no doubt seen to be good value, although they proved to be white elephants having a lifting capacity of only 4 1/2 tons. One was stored in the headshunt at Pilton Yard, coupled to a match truck built at Lancing Works in 1927. The other languished in Lynton goods yard.

The newness of Manning, Wardle 2-6-2T No. 188 LEW contrasts with the tired looking track and faded carriage paintwork in this view taken at Lynton in 1926. Delivered in July 1925, LEW was ordered by the S.R., perhaps as a replacement for the American Baldwin locomotive LYN. LEW was painted in full Maunsell olive green lined black and white with primrose yellow lettering, including painted buffer beam figures. The cab rear appears to be in olive green with black and white lining around the brass number plate. Note the poor condition of the L&BR track with rails held in place with dog spikes on sleepers that seem to be little more than faced logs. The carriages include two open centres, sandwiching brake composite No.17 which had been built by the L&BR in 1911.

*L&BR Manning Wardle
2-6-2 T locomotive EXE is
shown here on a Locomotive
Publishing Co. postcard of
circa 1913/14. Originally
built with an open bunker at
the rear, the locomotives
were modified by enclosing
the rear bunker and reducing
the overhanging cab front.
This card shows EXE shortly
after modification. The livery
is a dark green with orange
lining and black borders,
with red/brown underframes.
The outside Joy valve gear is
clearly shown.*

London & South Western & Lynton & Barnstaple Railways.

CHEAP TICKETS **ILFRACOMBE TO LYNTON.**

Commencing MONDAY, JULY 1st,

AND ON

EVERY WEEK-DAY DURING JULY, AUGUST & SEPTEMBER, 1907.

DAILY EXCURSIONS

TO

LYNTON

Via BARNSTAPLE TOWN will be run as under :

	TIMES.		Return Fare.
	a m	a m	
ILFRACOMBE (L. & S.W.R.) - - dep.	8 0	9 55	
BARNSTAPLE TOWN - - - - arr.	8 34	10 29	**4/-**
BARNSTAPLE TOWN (L.& B. R.) dep.	8 40	10 33	
LYNTON - - - - - - - - - - arr.	10 9	12 1	

RETURNING from Lynton daily at 5.0 p.m., arriving at Ilfracombe
at 7.20 p.m.; or at 6.15 p.m. from Lynton, arriving at
Ilfracombe at 8.31 p.m.

The L. & S.W.R. Route to Lynton via Barnstaple Town and L. & B.R. is most
picturesque, and affords splendid views of some of the finest scenery in Devon. Partly
open-sided Cars are in use on the L. & B.R., allowing Passengers to view the surrounding
country to best advantage.

Children under Three Years of age, Free.   Three to Twelve, Half-Fares.   No Luggage allowed.
The issuing of Through Tickets is subject to the conditions and regulations referred to in the Time Tables, Bills
and Notices of the respective Companies on whose Railway or Steamboats they are available; and the holder, by accepting
a Through Ticket, agrees that the respective Companies are not to be liable for any loss or damage, injury, delay or detention
caused or arising off their respective Railway or Steamboats.   The contract and liability of the Company are limited
to its own Railways and Steamboats.

TICKETS may be obtained at L. & S.W.R. Co.'s Office, 97, High Street, Ilfracombe.

R. D. & S.—31,368 10,000.   (2/2705)

CHAS. J. OWENS, General Manager, L. & S.W.R.
CHAS. E. DREWETT. General Manager, L. & B.R.

Above - *The Lynton bay platform at Barnstaple Town station on Wednesday 8th August 1923. There is little visible evidence of the Southern Railway's takeover of the L&BR earlier in the year. The carriage parked in the headshunt is L&BR number 11, an All Third supplied by Bristol Wagon & Carriage Works in 1898. It would be renumbered 2469 by the Southern Railway and appears here in an all over single colour livery. In the distance can be seen the L&BR signal box, a timber cabin supplied by Evans O'Donnell. The L&B line here crosses land reclaimed by filling in what was once a pleasure park with an ornamental lake surrounding a small island called 'Monkey Island'. The space to the right of the track is occupied by allotments. The area occupied by the signal cabin is now the site of the Barnstaple Civic Centre.*

Opposite bottom *- The L&BR closed on 29th September 1935 and the last train is seen here crossing Chelfham Viaduct, 4½ miles from Barnstaple. No. 188 LEW and No. 759 YEO double head the heavily patronised nine coach train. The viaduct was the largest piece of civil engineering on the L&B and was the largest viaduct ever built on the English narrow gauge, crossing the Stoke Rivers valley on eight arches of Marland brick. The viaduct was grade II listed in 1965 and still stands some 65 feet above the valley floor.*

Above - Lynton & Lynmouth terminus Wednesday 19th August 1931. Manning, Wardle No.760 EXE waits in the drizzle with the last up train of the day. The train comprises two coaches and a four year old 8-wheeled van delivered by J&F Howard in August 1927. The van still has its original timber 'X' bracing which would be replaced, because of rot, in 1934 with steel angle bracing. The locomotive has yet to be fitted with steam heating although the rear vacuum pipe has been re-routed and riveted plates fitted to the rear valance following modifications to the rear pony truck circa 1929. Note also the loco still carries an 'E' prefix above the number. The Manning, Wardles were originally built with equalising beams between the trailing and driving axle springs. These were removed and replaced with fixed spring hangers but for some reason the bolts for the equalising beam pivot were left in-situ on EXE and are clearly visible in this view.

Opposite - Looking north towards Lynton & Lynmouth terminus Wednesday 19th August 1931. The photographer has positioned himself so as to capture the replacement ex-L&SWR home and starting bracket signals installed by the Southern Railway on 2nd December 1924. Amongst other improvements carried out by the Southern was a new wooden prefabricated bungalow built for the stationmaster. In this rare view it is seen under construction on the embankment above the locomotive shed and was supplied by F. Pratten & Co. of Midsomer Norton. In the foreground is a good detail view of the upgraded S.R. trackwork which featured new sleepers and ballast, and clipped and bolted rails in place of the original L&BR dog spikes. The original rails were re-used. Note also the crude sleeper-built buffer stop on the siding. The terminus at Lynton was perched 700 feet above the twin town of Lynmouth, and some distance from Lynton.

Woody Bay looking south on Wednesday 19th August 1931. A Manning, Wardle is shunting the goods siding whilst 4-wheeled Bristol-built box van No. 47037 (ex-L&BR No. 4) is parked in the goods bay siding. Note the track in the foreground has been laid on concrete sleepers, whilst the signals have been replaced with S.R. rail-built examples. The buildings on the left were store sheds used for storing manures and feeds used by local farmers, and the doors have raised 'anti-vermin' thresholds. The building just left of the signal displayed a date of 1910 and all have now been demolished. The spindly structure furthest from the camera was a coal store used by a local coal merchant and coal wagons would be parked next to this store for unloading. The 1 in 50 gradient is clearly visible falling away in the distance.

Woody Bay looking north on Wednesday 19th August 1931. A Manning, Wardle has pulled clear of its two coach train with a wagon to be shunted into the goods siding. The Southern influence is seen in the new concrete name board, concrete fence panels, concrete telgraph pole and concrete lamp huts - all products of Exmouth Junction concrete works. In the distance the original and rarely photographed L&BR Evans O'Donnell timber post up home signal has yet to be replaced with a S.R. rail-built signal. The Brake Third carriage nearest the camera is S.R. No. 4108 (ex-L&BR No. 16). Note the box at the rear of the coach which contained a calcium carbide generator for the supply of acetylene gas to the carriage lamps.

Terry Cole's Rolling Stock File No. 21

SECR Saloons

We have looked in some depth at Maunsell coaches in previous issues so now for something completely different. The South Eastern and Chatham Railway like many pre-grouping companies seemed to build coaches to a myriad of differing designs. There were however, two features of which the SECR was particularly fond: the 'Saloon' and the brake coach with a 'Birdcage' lookout for the guard. We will consider the latter further in a future issue but this time we will look at some varieties of the SECR saloon coach.

Saloons were usually for first class passengers but there were some for 2nd class (later down-rated to 3rd) as well. Some coaches were short, some long whilst saloons also differed in length. There were also saloon brakes, picnic and invalid saloons and so on. It must have been a nightmare for the orderly Southern who liked interchangeable coach rakes of a standard composition. From 1909 rather more standardisation in coach production was effected with a large number of 3-coach 'Birdcage' sets being built for the outer suburban services.

This is No. S7357S, a bogie first with a saloon compartment seen at East Grinstead on 7 August 1956 probably in BR red livery. It is one of 11 similar coaches built by the Metropolitan Carriage & Wagon Co. in 1907/8 mainly for use on boat trains. Originally SECR No. 960, it has an overall length of 53ft 10in and seats 27. The SR allocated diagram 490. Seen from the end nearest the camera we have a 1st compartment, a pair of lavatories, a 1st saloon (length 19ft 9in) followed by two more 1st compartments with a pair of lavatories in-between. In later life it found itself in Set 920 and ended up making a daily return trip between the outer suburbs and the city. Withdrawal of these coaches started in the early 1940s. No. 7357 was the last survivor being withdrawn in December 1957.

No. S7919S is an unusual vehicle seen here at Eardley Road sidings on 17 September 1960 after withdrawal. It was one of three saloons built by the Met. R.C.& W.Co. in September 1905. All three vehicles were different. This vehicle (originally no 3785), had one saloon and two ordinary compartments and seated 20. Unusually it also had a corridor and gangways at both ends. Together with one of the other vehicles it was placed in the royal train. The Southern renumbered it No. 7919. At some time subsequently it was removed from the royal train becoming a first class invalid saloon with eight seats. As a corridor vehicle it acquired BR carmine and cream livery in which it is seen here. It was withdrawn in 1959.

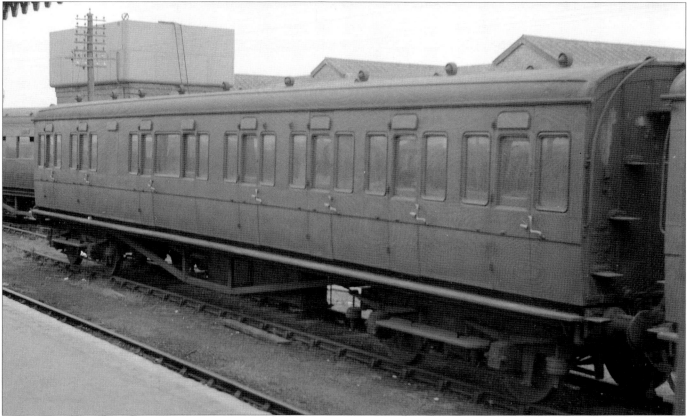

This photo shows ex SECR Composite No. S5499S at Paddock Wood on 25 February 1961. It was one of 10 bogie-first and second class coaches with a saloon, original number 1349, built between 1915 and 1920 as centre vehicles for the last SECR 3-coach sets. Although these retained the same interior layout and length (63ft 10½ in) as the previous 62 sets, there were no mouldings on the bodies and the brake vehicles were devoid of 'Birdcages'. Nearest the camera we have three originally 2nd class compartments followed by a 1st class compartment. Then there is the 1st class saloon (length 13ft 5in) followed by a pair of lavatories and then two more 1st class compartments. The coach was originally in SECR set No. 201 which became SR set No. 633. In 1956 together with No. S3542S it was converted to push-pull operation, the lavatories taken out of use and the windows sheeted over becoming set No.656. It was withdrawn in January 1962. [All photos David Wigley]

Stroudley B1 0-4-2 No. 198 *Sheffield* on the relief road at East Croydon station in 1904.
[Photographer: not known]

CROYDON LBSCR
Images from the Mike Morant collection

R. J. Billinton B2 class 4-4-0 No. 319 *John Fowler* on the relief road at East Croydon station in 1904.
[Photographer: not known]

R. J. Billinton B4 class 4-4-0 No. 45 *Bessborough* at East Croydon. *[Photographer: W. Hopkins-Brown]*

Stroudley D1 0-4-2T No. 263, in seemingly ex-works condition, is depicted facing south on the Up through road at East Croydon. Note the rarely photographed East Croydon Main running-in board in the background which is probably of SECR origin rather than LBSCR.
[Photographer: W. Hopkins-Brown]

The sole Stroudley D1X 0-4-2T No. A79 (or 79A as some people prefer) is depicted facing south on the Up through road at East Croydon.
[Photographer: W. Hopkins-Brown]

Another and much earlier shot of Billinton E5 class 0-6-2T No. 591 immaculately turned out and still bearing the name *TILLINGTON*. Note the 'Hall & Co. Chief Office' board in the background. *[Photographer: W. Hopkins-Brown]*

Stroudley G class 2-2-2 No. A.329 *Stephenson* storms through East Croydon Main in 1914 whilst hauling the Sunday Eastbourne Pullman. Although there's a general lack of sharpness to the central subject this image is of considerable interest. The number alone dates this negative to 1914 as the 'A' prefix was applied to indicate that the number duplicated that already in use on the recently built Lawson Billinton L class 4-6-4T. A.329 was already past her prime as she had already outlived the remainder of the class by some three years and this working, allegedly, was just about all she was used for by this time in her working life. The other point of note is that this is a rare example of an image taken at East Croydon that includes both an LBSCR loco and an SECR one during the pre-grouping era. *[Photographer: W. Hopkins-Brown]*

Above - Stroudley G class 2-2-2 No. A.329 *Stephenson* Takes a break at East Croydon in 1914. The number dates this negative to 1914 as the 'A' prefix was applied to indicate that the number duplicated that already in use on the recently built Lawson Billinton L class 4-6-4T. A.329 was already past her prime as she had already outlived the remainder of the class by some three years. *Below* - Marsh I3 class 4-4-2T No. 78 is the motive power for the down Southern Belle, later to become known as the Brighton Belle, as it enters East Croydon Main station. *[Photographer (both) : W. Hopkins-Brown]*

A sight to stir the imagination of any LBSCR aficianado is this one of Marsh J2 class 4-6-2T No. 326 Bessborough at East Croydon. Note that the carriage behind the bunker is a Pullman car. *[Photographer: W. Hopkins-Brown]*

Many regard the 4-6-4T wheel arrangement as the acme of balanced locomotive design and Marsh's L class epitomises all that is good about it. Here we see No. 332 awaiting departure from East Croydon Local facing in the direction of London. *[Photographer: W. Hopkins-Brown]*

Richard Billinton B4 class 4-4-0 No. 66 *Balmoral* at South Croydon. *[Photographer: not known]*

Billinton/Marsh B2X class 4-4-0 No. 318 accelerates through South Croydon station whilst in charge of the 4.30 pm Victoria - Brighton service on 30/7/21.*[Photographer: W. Hopkins-Brown]*

The prototype Marsh H2 class 4-4-2 No. 421 in photographic grey livery accelerates through South Croydon station. The balloon stock and clerestory Pullman cars are also worthy of note.

[Photographer: W. Hopkins-Brown]

(MORE TO FOLLOW - SOON!)

SOUTHERN RAILWAY STEAM BREAKDOWN CRANES
Part 2: SR CRANES
Peter Tatlow

Peter Tatlow, author of the acclaimed 2012 published *Railway Breakdown cranes – Volume 1*, concludes his exploration of the SR's examples. (Volume 2 will be available in January 2013.)

Upon amalgamation, the Southern Railway inherited ten steam breakdown cranes, two 36-ton cranes at Nine Elms and Salisbury; a pair of 20-ton at Exmouth Jct and Eastleigh; four 15-ton at Bournemouth, Brighton, New Cross and Ashford(K); and two 10-ton at Strawberry Hill and Guildford. An early review of the breakdown capacity available to the company must have identified that, with the 84 and 98 ton locomotives already in use, the Central and Eastern divisions were deficient in crane power. Steps had already been taken to order two more long-jib 36-ton cranes off Ransomes & Rapier similar to that supplied to the LSWR eight years earlier, when the catastrophe at Sevenoaks on 24 August 1927 emphasised the point. Although Ashford's 15-ton crane made a start to clear the debris, the two 36 ton cranes on the Western Division had to be brought in to handle the derailed 2-6-4 tank No 800 *River Cray*. On delivery later in the year, Nos 80S and 81S were allocated to Bricklayers Arms and Brighton, causing the 15-ton crane at Brighton to be cascaded to Ashford (Kent) and the existing one there sent to Stewarts Lane.

Another decade went by and the Southern invested in a further pair of 36-ton cranes, again from Ransomes & Rapier, but this time adopting a 4-axle carriage supported by Stokes Patent relieving system. This consisted of a pair of 4-wheel removable bogies, one at each end of the carriage, to assist in distributing the total weight of the crane while in train formation, thereby improving its route availability. Once on site, however, one or both of the bogies could be removed to enable the crane to approach closer to the load to be lifted. The new cranes were allocated to Nine Elms and Bricklayers Arms, causing their existing cranes to be moved to Fratton and Ashford (K), the latter's 15-ton crane going to Ramsgate.

Two years later the SR was the beneficiary of two 45-ton cranes, yet again from the Ipswich stable with relieving bogies, paid for by the Government as part of the ARP preparations. The GW received four similar, while the LNER's six were supplied by Cowans Sheldon to the same specification. Ransomes & Rapier went on to supply six more 45-ton cranes to the Ministry of Supply for use by the Army and two for the LNER. The Southern's were initially sent to sheds close to, but outside London, notably Feltham and Guildford from where they could be sent in to cope with air raid damage without being exposed to undue risk themselves. Guildford had been without a crane for some years, while Feltham was temporary host to No 1196S taking refuge from the bombing, but to which, nonetheless, it shortly returned.

There seems to have been some confusion as to whether they belonged to the Government, who paid for them, or the railway and they were not formally taken into stock until 23 December 1942. They were, nonetheless, from the outset manned by railwaymen and in the early days the cranes were employed extensively on war work. The latter included the use of three 45-ton cranes (including one from the LNER) changing the barrels of 14-inch naval guns installed at coastal batteries overlooking The Channel at St Margaret's-at-Cliffe, near Dover.

As the vast resources of military hardware was built up in preparation for D-Day and during the invasion of Europe, concerns must have been expressed at Exmouth Jct's puny 20-ton crane's ability to cope quickly with any serious obstruction of the line in the West Country. Authority was given for the Southern to purchase a further 45-ton crane but delivery was not made until late in 1945. In the meantime by July 1944 Salisbury's 36-ton crane

Opposite top - *36-ton Ransomes & Rapier steam crane No. DS80 of 1927 at Woking on 21 April 1967, having recently arrived from Guildford to deal with a pair of new 50-ton Whale ballast wagons which had run away and ploughed through the buffer stops ending up buried in the ramp to platform 2. (Author [35/79-3])*

Opposite bottom - *The next pair of 36-ton cranes again from Ransomes & Rapier adopted relieving bogies, but were otherwise similar, with 4-wheel instead of bogie match wagons. Ds1197 was photographed beneath a canopy beside Bricklayers Arms shed in early BR days. (Lens of Sutton, author's collection)*

seems to have been temporarily loaned to Exmouth Jct, while until sometime prior to June 1945 Salisbury's work was covered by a War Department 45-ton crane.

With the arrival of the new crane and with the war over a reassessment of the disposition of cranes was undertaken and a general post instigated amongst almost all of them between April and June 1946, including the withdrawal of the 15-ton Dunlop & Bell No 32S.

Postscript. It was to be well into the BR period before the Southern Region received any more breakdown cranes. As part of the Modernisation Plan a dozen 75-ton and ten-30 ton cranes were obtained from Cowans Sheldon and, whereas those for the other regions were again steam-powered, the two 75-ton and two 30-ton intended for the Southern were diesel-powered. Their arrival and the beginning of a general retrenchment led to the withdrawal of all the remaining 15-and 20-ton steam cranes on the Region and the redistribution of the rest. Although both the 30 ton cranes went to the Western Division (Bournemouth and Feltham) in the summer of 1962, it was two years until one 75-ton joined them, being stationed at Nine Elms, the other going to Hither Green on the Eastern Division. A couple of years later, however, Eastleigh and Hither Green exchanged cranes.

Conclusion. With adjustments to regional boundaries, the Western Region had already gained Exmouth Jct's 45-ton

crane, while with completion of the Bournemouth Electrification Scheme in July 1967, Salisbury's 36-ton also migrated to the Western, being down-rated to 32-tons and sent as their No 376 first to Worcester and then Landore, Swansea. Apart from a nasty accident to No Ds1196 when it overturned at Brighton on 25 October 1964, and was subsequently cut up and replaced by sister No DS1197, the remaining SR cranes had surprisingly long careers. Other than the above two, all the rest went on to receive CEPS numbers in the late '70s. They continued to serve the Region until former 76-and 50 tonne steam cranes from other regions, converted to diesel power, became available to fulfil the heavy lifting requirements of the rationalised breakdown arrangements in the post loose-coupled wagon age. Upon withdrawal, four went on to be acquired for preservation. Although sadly one of these has quite recently made its way to the breaker's yard, three remain on heritage railways.

Further details of these and all British standard gauge breakdown cranes will be found in a two volume work by the author, the first of which was published by Noodle Books early in 2012.

Note: The dates it is thought a crane was first allocated to a depot are shown in upright letters where a crane is merely known to have been at a depot on a specific date(s) are shown in italics.

Opposite page - *Eastleigh's 45-ton Ransomes & Rapier steam breakdown crane No Ds1560 unloads a delivery of pre-tensioned concrete beams into temporary storage at Havant goods yard on 4 January 1966, prior to their eventual use in the reconstruction of the road approach viaduct to Portsmouth Harbour station. (Author [35/66-3])*

Above - *The final breakdown crane acquired by the SR was another 45-ton from Ransomes & Rapier delivered towards the end of 1945 and sent to Exmouth Jct, where it remained until after the Western Region took over at the beginning of 1963. Here it is clearing up re-railed wagons at Coaxden Bridge, Axminster on 7 March 1973. (AE West, courtesy MS King [R5858])*

Right - *Cowans Sheldon diesel hydraulic 75-ton breakdown crane No DB965186 from Wimbledon Park in a siding at Chertsey on 3 June 1970. (Author [35/97-32])*

Southern Railway Ransomes & Rapier Steam Breakdown Cranes

Cap'ty / Date delv'd	Running No		Match wagon No SR/BR	Allocation	Disposal
	SR/ 1st BR	BR-CEPS			
36T/ 1927	80S/ DS80	ADRR 95225	80SM/ DS3087	Bricklayers Arms 10/27, Ashford (K) 5/38, Guildford 6/62, Stewart's Lane (spare) 7/67-1/79	Scrapped at Stewart's Lane 3/86
36T/ 1927	81S/ DS81	ADRR 95201	81SM/ DS3088	Brighton 11/27-5/38, Fratton 6/46-'58, Guildford 8/4/59-23/4/60, Feltham 10/60 Stewart's Lane 2/63-11/86	Wdn 9/9/86. Sold to K&ESR 1/87
36T/ 1937	1196S/ DS1196	-	1196SM/ DS3092	Nine Elms 11/37, Feltham 10/5/40 (tempy), Nine Elms 10/42, Brighton 6/46, overturned 25/10/64	Cut up 10/64
36T/ 1937	1197S/ DS1197	-	1197SM/ DS3093	Bricklayers Arms 12/37, Hither Green 20/2/62, Brighton 25/10/64-'70, Stewarts Lane 30/6/79	Wth'n 11/78
45T/ 11.7.40	1560S/ DS1560	ADRR 95209	1560SM/ DS3094	Feltham 8/40, Nine Elms 6/46, Eastleigh '64-4/1/66, Hither Green 11/86, Stewarts Lane OOU 4/88,	Sold to Swindon RE 6/89, cut up 2010 at Halesowen
45T/ 23.7.40	1561S/ DS1561	ADRR 95210	1561SM/ DS3095	Guildford 8/40, Ashford (K) 6/62, Chart Leacon 31/10/67-16/7/77, Brighton 5/78-11/86, Stewarts Lane 4/88	Sold to Swindon RE 6/89, Southall 1/11
45T/ c11.45	1580S/ DS1580, WR 151	ADRR 95216	1580SM/ DS3096	Exmouth Jct 11/45-11/64, to WR 1/1/63, Newton Abbot 8/65-7/69, Laira 1/72-1/79, Old Oak Common	Sold to Glouc Wks Rly 11/83

Cowans Sheldon Cranes acquired for Southern Region by BR

Cap'ty / Date delv'd	Running No		Match wagon No SR/BR	Allocation	Disposal
30T/ 1962	DB 965183	ADRC 96100	DB 998530	Feltham 6/62- 9/69, Clapham Jct 1/9/70, CMEE 5/4/73 Horsham 25/9/77 to 4/01, Doncaster Electrification Construction Depot 4/03-07/05, Carnforth 22/02/06	Extant Carnforth OOU 4/4/11
30T/ 1962	DB 965184	ADRC 96101	DB 998531	Bournemouth 9/62- 9/69, CMEE 29/1/74, Horsham 9/80 to 9/04. Lyndney 11/06/05-03/08.	Scrapped by Booths, Rother-ham
75T/ 1964	DB 965185	ADRC 96200	DB 998532	Hither Green 5/64, Eastleigh 4/65 to 20/4/75, Chart Leacon 5/78 to 3/95, OOU Ashford 3/97.	Sold to Phillips, cut up 2-3/98
75T/ 1964	DB 965186	ADRC 96201	DB 998533	Nine Elms c8/64, Wimbledon Park 7/67 to 9/80, Eastleigh c'86, Ashford Repair Crane Depot 4/88, Stewarts Lane c'88 to 2/91, Ashford Plant Depot OOU 9/94.	Source of spares. Sold to Phillips, cut up 2-3/98

'REBUILT' - THE LETTERS AND COMMENTS PAGES

We apologise this time for the shorter than intended final section, despite the increased number of pages in this issue we have somehow contrived still to run short - and there are also a number of articles held over. So without wasting space on excuses we start with some comments and a request from our dear friend Fred Emery.

"The new catalogue is almost a book in itself. I look forward to LMS Wartime (Can we mention that in SW? – too late now) mainly because by various means I got hold of the Southern ABC and went down to Balham station, where the first two engines to come through, both on freight, were a Super D and an 8F, and of course their numbers were not in the ABC. 'Stupid book', I thought, not being immediately aware of the through workings that existed between the SR and elsewhere.

"I think the frontispiece (SW20) is superb, alright so probably a picture of the lady on holiday, but what a wonderful illustration. Such a pity the original L & B line did not survive.

"In the same issue, page 8 could this bogie guard's van already be in departmental use? Page 55, most unusual and full of interest. Might this even be an experiment that would eventually lead to the SR Electric locos? The J class tanks, most interesting but I think it was found most of their

duties could be covered by the smaller 'H' type although it must be said the latter did have a smaller bunker capacity.

"Going back now to SW19, the 'O1' at Balham tickled the grey cells, the tree has long gone but the pub is still there . Referring still to Balham, I recall seeing an ex WD 2-8-0 heading up to Streatham Hill but oh so grubby I could not even make out the number.

"Also from Fred a query which we hope someone may be able to answer. An ancestor was involved in the building of the tunnels in the Norwood of south-east London area. As was the procedure at the time explosive was often used which on this occasion did not go off as expected. In such cases they would then wait a stipulated period of time before investigating further. Of course what happened was the explosive then detonated killing at least one man – whether immediately or in consequence of injury is not known. The family have been unable to locate a death certificate although some idea of dates of tunnel building or accidents in their construction might help. Any replies would be appreciated."

Now from Jeremy Clarke, "Hi Kevin, re your note about info on this vehicle in SW no19. There's a quite full description in David Gould's 'Bulleid's SR Steam Passenger Stock', Oakwood." *Jeremy - appreciated of course, but apart from the above has anyone any more illustrations of No. 100S - Ed.*

Glen Woods has also been in correspondence with Nick Stanbury over his (Glen's) recent article on Milk Tanks. NS - The timing and the route of the 3.24 (or 3.26) pm East Croydon – Wood Lane milk empties in the late 1950s seems unclear and not in accordance with all of the four photos of this working. GW - The main problem with the timings was the fact that the Railway kept changing them. For some periods the train was the 3 24 p.m. from East Croydon on Weekdays and at others 3.24 p.m. Mondays to Fridays and 3. 26 p.m. on Saturdays. All J.J. Smiths photographs were taken on Saturdays hence the mixture of 3. 24 and 3. 26 in the captions. The train was normally routed via the Brighton Main line with diversions via other routes when necessary. NS - But the headcode is wrong in that there should also be a disc above the right buffer; it is a coincidence that (as displayed) it appears to be the Waterloo – CJ code I mentioned before! GW - he headcode is incorrect but there does not appear to be a reason for it. Also of note is the fact that this was a Bricklayers Arms locomotive - it may have been a hasty replacement for the booked locomotive. NS - I note from the Bluebell archive that John Smith noted the train time as 3.34, so I guess your reference to 3.24 is an error. GW - John Smith did not note the train as 3 34, his photograph collection was acquired after he passed away and subsequently uploaded by a Bluebell Railway Museum member. We have now checked JJ Smith's original negative envelope at the archive and can confirm that he recorded the train as the 3 24 p.m. The Bluebell Museum site has been updated.

Now from Keith Withers on Stationary boilers - "Reference to the recent article on Stationary Boilers, I note there is no record of the boiler that was sited in the Carriage Sheds at Southampton Western / New Docks. These docks were built on reclaimed land by the Southern Rly. during the 1920/30s and a storage/servicing facility for Boat train coaching stock provided. To enable pre-heating of stock a ex L&BSCR loco boiler No 65 built 1892 was installed 2/1/1935. This boiler was removed and sent Eastleigh for a new firebox to be fitted 27/6/1952, however on inspection in the Boiler shop it was condemned and a replacement returned on 17/11/1952 and commissioned 1/1/ 1953. Boiler No S/305 ex Drummond class S11 No 30403, having been rebuilt but retaining original barrel 10/1931.

"This boiler continued in use until the early 60s when with the withdrawal the USA tank shunting engines and their replacement by Ruston Hornsby diesel shunters not having steam heating facilities during stock transfers, five carriage heating vans were provided. These could be attached to boat train stock and taken to the required departure berths whilst remaining operational, they had a 2-cylinder RH diesel generator and Spanner boiler and were push button operated externally by staff. Boiler S/305 was sold and cut up on site during the late 60s by a scrap metal contractor.

"Ref USA tank 30068, It was usual for an engine from the docks MPD to be requested by the BR Marine dept to provide steam during the winter lay-ups/refits mainly for onboard fuel oil tank cleaning duties along side the berth/ dry dock, these Locos were attended by a member of the shed staff. The regulator handle was removed.

"Ref Bulleid Pacifics safety valve testing Eastleigh Works. It was standard practice for SVs to be overhauled and hydraulically tested in the Fitting shop and every three weeks or so when suitable amount were ready they would be taken out to the test house where a Bulleid with its higher WP, awaiting works attention would be connected to the test rig and each valve set to the required working pressure and sealed to prevent tampering. The loco would have previously been fitted with a higher rated SV. I hope this will be of interest."

Now from Richard Jones reference 'Singleton' (SW16), "Some comments on train movements and timetables inspired by examination of the photos in

And of course like buses, not just one relevant image, following on from page 77 of SW No 20, but two (see over as well). Here we see the 13 coach 'Farnborough Flyer' arriving at Farnborough from Basingstoke having reversed direction at the latter point. The train had arrived at Basingstoke from Bradford behind a GNR 4-4 -2, SR Nos. 31806 and 32329 responsible for the final leg of the journey. Michael E Ware

The GN 'Atlantic' and GCR 'Director' are seen being serviced at Basingstoke, turned and ready for the return. The former LNER observation car has also been turned and awaits reattaching to the return working.

SW16. Firstly congratulations to Denis Caiger for an excellent article on Singleton. As part of educating myself on Brighton signalling practice so that I can operate my projected model authentically, if I ever get around to building it, I have been studying the signalling diagram and working timetables and would offer the following observations on the captions of a couple of the photographs.

"Middle photo page 15 – Up train in Down loop platform, this is a widely reproduced photo, which I understand was taken by E R Lacey, the presence of a C2X suggests a goods working, and the shadow of the station name-board indicates it is the morning. The latest working timetable I have (courtesy of Geoff Smith) is one dated 12/06/1922 to 01/10/1922, which shows an up goods working arriving at Singleton 10:40, with plenty of time for shunting as it doesn't depart until 11:35. This could be signalled into the down loop by stopping the train at the up home signal and then using what appears to be a calling on signal operated by south box lever no. 25. the points operated by South box 19 and 13 (cross over down to up, and down main/loop exits) have facing point locks operated by South box levers 18 and 20, which only potentially leaves the turntable point (South box 12), if entering the down loop, or the facing cross over (South box 15) if entering the down main, as facing points to traverse, without FPLs – I am not familiar enough with LBSC/SR signalling practice to know whether this would require them to be clipped, however it should be noted that in various combinations, South box points 12, 14, 15, 17, 19 & 21 are locked/released by the North Box levers 9, 11 & 12, and I would guess that this might satisfy operating rules. (Did the Brighton use economy FPLs where a single lever operated and locked the points?) I would suggest that the (up) goods train (once in possession of the single line staff) could be

hand signalled away from the up loop, with entry to the single line section controlled by the advanced starter operated by north Box lever 8 (which might also be the limit of shunt?) The above (operational) constraints I postulate would also apply to getting the (up) Royal train into the Down main platform (photo top of page 12) and away northwards

"Referring back to the Lacey picture, you may also notice that the down main home signal (North Box 28, slotted with South Box 1) is off, and I would suggest that this heralds the arrival of 11.31 down train (ex 10.50 Pulborough, due Chichester 11.45), after which the C2X can proceed to Petworth (arr.1.56), pausing to shunt at Midhurst (arr. 12.02, dep. 1.11) and Selham (arr. 1.19, dep. 1.47).

"The locking of various points and slotting of signals between the two boxes would have kept the signalman very busy on the majority of days when the south box was not permanently manned.

"Whilst on the subject of train movement at Singleton, both Ian Serallier in "All change at Singleton" and Smith/Mitchell in "Branch lines to/around Midhurst" refer to school trains crossing at Singleton – does anyone have any further information on this, as the only passenger trains which appear to have crossed at Singleton were around 9.00 am (with a few minutes variations over the years) which seems a bit late for a school service to me, and even this had been discontinued by 1922.

"Any other thoughts or comments on Singleton would be greatly appreciated, particular a photograph of the turntable."

More next time - promise - Ed!